W.H Dallinger

The Creator and what we may know of the method of creation

W.H Dallinger

The Creator and what we may know of the method of creation

ISBN/EAN: 9783743463622

Manufactured in Europe, USA, Canada, Australia, Japa

Cover: Foto ©Thomas Meinert / pixelio.de

Manufactured and distributed by brebook publishing software (www.brebook.com)

W.H Dallinger

The Creator and what we may know of the method of creation

THE CREATOR,

AND WHAT WE MAY KNOW OF THE METHOD OF CREATION.

THE FERNLEY LECTURE OF 1887.

BY

W. H. DALLINGER, LL.D., F.R.S.

> 'For I have learned
> To look on Nature, not as in the hour
> Of thoughtless youth. . . . And I have felt
> A presence that disturbs me with the joy
> Of elevated thoughts; a sense sublime
> Of something far more deeply interfused,
> Whose dwelling is the light of setting suns,
> And the round ocean and the living air,
> And the blue sky, and in the mind of man:
> A motion and a spirit, that impels
> All thinking things, all objects of all thought,
> And rolls through all things.'
> — WORDSWORTH.

Ninth Thousand.

LONDON:
T. WOOLMER, 2, CASTLE STREET, CITY ROAD, E.C.,
AND 66, PATERNOSTER ROW, E.C.

1888.

TO

JAMES S. BUDGETT, Esq.,

IN REMEMBRANCE OF

A FRIENDSHIP

WHICH HAS INFLUENCED BENEFICENTLY

MUCH OF HIS LIFE AND WORK;

THIS LITTLE VOLUME

IS AFFECTIONATELY INSCRIBED BY

THE AUTHOR.

PREFACE.

The following discourse was prepared as a lecture. With the exception of the insertion of passages which it was found necessary to omit in delivery, on account of too great length, it is printed as it was spoken. It addressed, and in its present form addresses, thoughtful and earnest minds, not concerned specially with questions of philosophy, metaphysics, and science, but alive to the advanced knowledge and thought of our times, and anxious to know, so far as in such a form it could be expressed, how the great foundation of religious belief, the existence of Deity, is affected by the splendid advance of our knowledge of nature. To have written more than the following pages contain, in answering this desire, would have necessitated what I have earnestly endeavoured to avoid, a change from a discourse into a treatise. It is hoped that, as it is presented, it may to some extent be found useful to those who sought it— not so much students, as men interested in the deeper thought of our age, but whose time is occupied with the labours and engagements of a busy life.

W. H. DALLINGER.

WESLEY COLLEGE, SHEFFIELD,
September 1, 1887.

THE CREATOR, AND WHAT WE MAY KNOW OF THE METHOD OF CREATION.

IN spite of the lucid and far-reaching reasoning of Hume, which aimed at effacing causality from our conceptions of phenomena, and making invariable sequence supplant it; in spite of Auguste Comte's stern effort to 'get rid of the vain pretension to investigate the causes of phenomena,' and the affirmation that 'forces are only movements, produced or tending to produce;' nay, in spite of all the logical effort of all the following years, there remains unaltered, that inalienable property of the human mind, consciousness of power; the ability to realize 'I can' simultaneously with 'I am.' In this originates our universal explanation of external phenomena. Because we can act and produce phenomena, we infer that all phenomena were inevitably produced by some transcendent but equivalent act of conscious power. If we think of a plane surface or a sphere, we can only think of them as occupants of space: so, if we think of the light beams of Sirius, or the motion of Mars, we realize the normal necessity of thinking of them ultimately as caused. This is an inevitable sequence of our consciousness, reason, and experience. A phenomenon appearing in time evokes the mental demand for something which is not that phenomenon, but without which it would not have existed.

In this lies the insatiable desire of mind to peer into the origin of, and reason for, the existence of this universe. Deepening knowledge brings broader light and expanding mystery, but this only quickens the intellectual purpose of the race to seek to solve the problem, why we are circled with the splendid phenomena of heaven and earth, and possessed of the mystery of ourselves?

But to meet this mental demand is no part of the business of science. The study of phenomena, their succession and their classification, is the essential work of science. It has no function, and is possessed of no instrument with which to look behind or below the sequence, in quest of some higher relation. The eye and the mind of the experimentalist know only of antecedent and consequent. These fill the whole circle of his research; let him find these, and he has found all. But since a cause is no more a phenomenon, than a thought is a material manifestation, that which fills the whole circumference claimed by science does *not* fill all the area legitimately held by reason. A prevision of the order, and the methods of the changes of the universe, is the ideal of science. But mind in its entirety refuses to be locked within such limits. It looks deeper than sequences, and farther back than phenomena; it demands, by the very laws of its existence, their cause. A continuity of transformed causes undoubtedly explains a wide, and ever-widening area of sequences. But that cannot annul the demand of reason for causation. It simply drives it farther back, and higher up, and indicates that the modes of action and relation originated by the

know of the Method of Creation. 3

primal cause are only the more sublimely rhythmic. Count this a lingering survival of 'mere metaphysics' who will, it is withal so stalwart, so perennial in our consciousness, amidst all vicissitudes of knowledge and reasoning, that whatever science may do, philosophy must give it audience.

The researches of science, then, are physical. The observable, finite contents of space and time are the subjects of its analysis. Existence, not the cause of existence, succession, not the reason of succession, method, not the origin of method, are the subjects of physical research. A primordial cause cannot be the subject of experiment nor the object of demonstration. It must for ever transcend the most delicate physical reaction, the profoundest analysis, and the last link in the keenest logic. Absolute knowledge concerning it can only be the prerogative of itself.

But human reason is not only, and wholly, concerned with the brilliant records of physical enquiry: it is conscious of powers within itself that transcend and elude all the processes of physics, and the analyses of mathematics. The activities of the mind are not exhausted, the demands of the mind are not met, the persistent questions of reason are not answered, by all the processes, all the products, and all the possibilities of physical research combined.

Science refuses absolutely to recognise mind as the primal cause of the sequences of matter. This is just;—within the strict region of its research; for phenomena, their sequences and classification, are its sole domain. But observe, science, universally, puts *force* where the reason asks for cause. The forces affecting matter, are tacitly assumed to be competent to account for every activity, every sequence, every phenomenon, and all the harmonies of universal being. A nexus for the infinite diversities and harmonies, a basis for all the equilibrium of nature, is found by modern science in force. But force is as absolutely inscrutable as mind. Force can never be known in itself; it is known by its manifestations. It is not a phenomenon; it produces phenomena. We cannot know it; but we know nothing without it.

Then the ultimate analysis of physical science is the relations of force and matter. But force is a subject of knowledge to science only in its manifestations; that is, motion. In irreducible terms, therefore, the final analysis of science is *matter as affected by motion.* These—matter and motion—are held by many advanced physicists to be the primary elements of all phenomena; the most minute, subtile, and occult reaction, and the most majestic cosmic manifestation are held to be explained by these. Thus the whole cosmos, with its infinite complexities and harmonies, arose in space, and is in space, because of the affections of matter by motion. To search out the motions on which all changes are based, to reduce all the activities of the universe, from the awful movement of a constellation, to the rhythmic swing of an atom; from the origin of mind, and the writing of Faust, to the building of a snow crystal, or the production of a flower, to sheer mechanics—matter affected by motion—is held to be the chief mission of science.

But examine for a moment the nature of the problem. The matter with which analysis is thus finally concerned cannot be matter as we know it. It is the existing *properties* or *qualities* of matter that affect us. Matter is hard, it is yellow, it is sweet. Now the very qualities that *make* matter as we know it are demonstrated by modern science to be but 'modes of motion;' matter is hot because the ultimate atoms of it vibrate in a special manner. The yellowness of an object is not in *it*, but in our percipient faculty. That which is yellow emits certain light vibrations only; these affect the retina in a special manner, and this affection we call the perception of yellowness. It is thus with all the qualities of matter.

Then what can that 'matter' be with which the physicist must ultimately and in the beginning deal? When matter is divested of all its qualities, divested in thought of all the 'modes of motion' by which it manifests itself to us, what is it? Is it mass, wholly incapable of affecting our senses? Matter *sine perceptione*? That cannot be a thing, it is an abstraction, and he must be something more than a bold man, who would logically infer an actual factor, corresponding to the abstract conception.

Manifestly, then, physical science and its methods cannot illuminate and explain all the dilating area of space, and flow of time, with which our consciousness and reason are concerned. Shapes and motion, form and number, are not data that can carry us to the origin of the universe. You must import an unacknowledged factor. Force stands ready: if you endow *it*, in imagination equipped in the uniform of science, with the very qualities of mind, no doubt you may cross the boundary of experimental science, and see in matter affected by motion the possibility of all that is. But, says Professor Huxley, '*Kraft und Stoff*—

force and matter—are paraded as the Alpha and Omega of existence. This, I apprehend, is the fundamental article of the faith materialistic, and whosoever does not hold it is condemned by the more zealous of the persuasion (as I have some reason to know) to the Inferno appointed for fools and hypocrites. But all this,' he continues, 'I heartily disbelieve; and . . . I will briefly give my reasons for persisting in my infidelity. In the first place, . . . it seems to me pretty plain that there is a third thing in the universe, to wit, consciousness, which, in the hardness of my heart or head, I cannot see to be matter, or force, or any conceivable modification of either, however intimately the manifestations of the phenomena of consciousness may be connected with the phenomena known as matter and force. In the second place, the arguments used by Descartes and Berkeley to show that our certain knowledge does not extend beyond our states of consciousness, appear to me to be as irrefragable now as they did when I first became acquainted with them, some half-century ago. All the materialistic writers I know of, who have tried to bite that file, have simply broken their teeth. But if this is true, our one certainty is the existence of the mental world; and that of *Kraft und Stoff* falls into the rank of, at best, a highly probable hypothesis.'[1]

Look, then, at the striking incongruity. With no explanation of matter without qualities; with no indication of how motion could arise and become rhythmic and infinitely harmonious; with the distinct knowledge that, when the physicist wants to demonstrate matter, he is compelled to do it in terms of motion; and, when he would prove the

[1] *Fortnightly Review*, No. ccxl., new series, December 1886, p. 794.

presence of motion, he can only do it in terms of matter; with all these fetters to our mental movement, and clouds before our eyes, it is argued that, by carrying the discoverable and apparently self-acting affections of matter by motion far enough back, we can explain the origin and structure of the universe.

I would repeat, that in such a mental effort, it is vain to seek logical aid from the employment of the word 'force.' We have seen that the only scientific idea of force we can ever have, is motion. Motion is the result of ever-varying relations, borne to each other by matter, space, and time. At a given instant a body is here; in a measurable interval after. it is not here, but yonder. 'Motion' carries with it no occult constructive power. It is change of place, and no more.

Is it not inevitable, then, that the mind should refuse its sanction to the claim, that 'the problem of the universe' is solved by these feeble factors ? 'If I were forced,' writes Professor Huxley, ' to choose between Materialism and Idealism, I should elect for the latter;'[1] and truly, if our choice must be between them, this is the normal alternative.

The loftiest object of human thought is to discover how far the material universe is an expression of supreme unity, of rhythmic activity, and of rational order. But for this, the mind must take a range that transcends, without limit, all physical sequences, laws, phenomena. Taking the broad basis of our consciousness and reasoning faculties, we must *relate* sequences, *interpret* phenomena, and, however remotely and imperfectly, endeavour to account for 'laws.' But in doing this we must remember that we have pushed

[1] *Fortnightly Review*, December 1886, p. 796.

our way beyond the last outpost of *physical* research. We have passed beyond the region where 'quod erat demonstrandum' is used. We have threaded our mental path into solitudes where no electrometer will be responsive, no spectroscope analytical, no lens revealing. We have come to the edge of all that we *know* and can *demonstrate;* and then, impelled by the moral and rational light within us, we judge and balance all that we know, and all that we are, and we reach, not a demonstration, for that cannot be, but a conviction, a moral and intellectual certainty, of the being of a primordial cause, which is second, in its firmness and security, to nothing within the area of mind.

Since the time of Newton and Leibnitz the laws of ordinary dynamics have been settled; but between dynamics, and the so-called 'imponderable forces,' by which it was assumed that an explanation was furnished of heat, chemical action, electricity, magnetism and the rest, there was a great gulf. That has been bridged over by a common measure of value, giving rise to a general dynamic law of all the forces of the universe. This is known as the 'Conservation of Energy.' It demonstrates, with more or less completeness, that all physical phenomena are the different appearances resulting from different groupings of matter by force. Both matter and force are eternally changeless in quantity. They can be neither diminished nor increased, neither created nor destroyed. The 'modes of motion' that produce the varied phenomena are interchangeable. Light may become heat, heat may become electricity; but there is no loss. When motion seems to disappear, it is only transferred into another mode. The phenomena of light, heat, electricity, result from changes wrought in matter by motion. Every ray of sunshine, for instance, is an interwoven group of powerful energies. Whence do they come? From changes in the matter of the sun. For every measure of sunshine received by the earth an equivalent measure of solar matter has been changed. Through the sunbeam the varied forms of energy produced in the sun have been received, and stored up on this earth. For incalculable centuries the world has been clothed with abundant vegetation. This will only grow in sunlight. The energies in the sunbeam act on living matter, as on a spore or a seed, causing it to grow. That is to say, under the influence of vital action, the forces of the sunbeam are changed into wood. A section from a pine mast, or an oak trunk, stands for a measurable quantity of sunshine. But coal is wood; forests buried and carbonized. Coal then has, as it were, fixed the energies of the sunbeams that poured upon the earth millions of years ago. Put coal where it will be in contact with oxygen and heat, and what follows? You get heat, light, chemical action; that is to say, the locked-up energies of the sunbeams of a measureless past are set free.

Here then, all the activity of the universe, every phenomenon, and every vibration of every atom, from the centre to the margin of the immeasurable whole, is directly related to a unity of primal power. Nothing has happened to-day in the remotest or nearest part of creation, but was linked in an unbroken chain to the first throb that thrilled the incipient universe in the mystery of 'the beginning.' Nothing is isolated through all duration and all space. Because, everywhere and always, the resulting phenomena are self-acting and rhythmic to our mode of research, shall we say that they have no cause, or that they have determined their own condition? because we find that the self-adjustments and sublimity of Nature, transcend infinitely all the conceptions of earlier generations, will it be logical to argue, that therefore Nature may be the more readily explained as causeless and devoid of mind? that, being self-adjusting and self-acting, it needed no cause? or shall we not the rather realize that this unbroken line of physical continuity and interaction through all duration to 'the beginning' brings us *there*, face to face, with the inscrutable Power, by which that unchanging unity and continuity of purposeful action was caused?

Every phenomenon is motion; motion can only begin in force. Within the range of human experience and thought, as it has been long without answer contended, there is no force known but *will:* could any other cause than the volition of a mind, have primarily directed force to affect matter so as to produce, for ever, the infinite harmonies and self-adjusting interactions of this vast Universe?

The very intellect, which finds so noble a vocation in the researches of science, and which is so brilliantly employed in penetrating into, and opening up, the *intelligibility* of the physical universe; and by that means demonstrating the *congruousness* of the cosmos; is the same intellect that is conscious of *itself*, and of its *power;* which knows itself as possessed of causative capacity; and which has absolutely no other source of knowledge concerning power, save that which arises in itself. The very rationality of the Creation, in our deepest analysis and broadest survey of it, leads the mind, by the conditions inseverable from its reasoning faculties, to see in its perfect relations the inevitable congruity of an intelligent cause. And all this, be it observed, results *after* science has disclosed the splendid treasures of its knowledge, the beauty and indisputable accuracy of its methods, and the new senses with which it has endowed itself by its instruments. Yes; the mind goes out to this conclusion, not defiant of science, but gratefully paying toll to it for an infinitely enlightening and ennobling passage through the marvels of phenomena, and the splendour of Nature's methods, right to the very margin, beyond which science herself declares she cannot go; and although the physicist may declare he does not need it, and the mathematician that he can dispense with it, although all their immediate problems can be worked without it, yet the mind goes forth on the wings of its rational powers, its moral consciousness, its judgment; and leaving the margin of matter, it seeks audience, as it were, with the very mystery that enshrouds the universe; and it rises to the conviction that its quest has not been vain; it has realized, dimly, imperfectly, and, as it were, faint with awe, the necessity of the presence and action of Eternal Mind.

No search into the relations of matter and motion can ever affect our consciousness of causality. We cannot be conscious of our own being without being simultaneously conscious that whatever begins to be, must have a cause, a reason, for its being. The very validity of our mental acts is imperilled, if the congruity of the principle of causality be doubted. Permit an illustration: a minute and beautiful crystal of unknown nature is before us. By a mental necessity we know—we cannot free ourselves from the conviction—that this crystal occupied a measurable time to become a crystal, and that being such, it occupies a measurable portion of space. May we rely on this fundamental act of mind? Is it truth? If not, there is not a mental act that ever was, or ever can be, veritable. But if it be true, then, since for man to produce a physical effect involves (1) the consciousness of *power* to do it, and (2) the volitional exercise of that power; and since the human mind is absolutely without a trace of knowledge of any other way in which power can be exercised, in earth or heaven; is not the insistence of reason that there must be a cause for cosmic phenomena, a mental act of the *same order* as that which insists on time and space as inseverable factors in the origin and existence of a crystal?

Causality in its mere mechanical relations may be considered for convenience, and translated as, 'mechanical law:' contemplated in its relation to a living organism, we may render it by such an expression as a 'law of life.' But carry causality to its spring, trace it back to consciousness and thought, and it admits of no disguise; it is power, it is volition; there is no halting in its phrase; it is, 'I can,' 'I will.'

Herbert Spencer himself affirms, ' The force by which we ourselves produce changes, and which serves to symbolize the causes of changes in general, is the final disclosure of analysis.'[1] 'I can,' 'I am able,' is a knowledge that emerges within us simultaneously with 'I am.' It involves a consciousness of power, which is the essence of causality. We possess it, in precisely the same way as we possess ourselves, or our thoughts. Our knowledge of power is not even derived from effort or resistance. We know as clearly what we mean by 'I am able,' as we do when we affirm 'I am here.' Being able, and *knowing* we are able, are

[1] *First Principles*, § 50, pp. 169, 170.

absolutely different. A telephone is mechanically able to transmit vocal sounds and language. But how different to man, who is not only able, but knows that he is able. This knowledge of our power to act is the immutable foundation of our belief in causation.

We may make two separate affirmations: as, for example, that 'the thermometer is 6° F. below zero,' and that 'water has become solid;' or, again, we may state, 'my fingers rest upon the key-board of an organ,' and 'now they move, and a symphony of Beethoven's is floating in the air.' These are 'sequences;' but is that enough? No. Instantly the mental act that *interprets* them is supplied. In both cases, our consciousness and reason are compelled to demand the exercise of power, by means of which one event succeeds the other. We are absolutely and irresistibly certain, in the latter case, that it must be so. A direct act of volition changed the fingers from rest into rhythmic motion, causing the organ to pour out music; and, by an intellectual necessity, we see that a diminished temperature, and frozen water, are not sequences merely; they must be related: and this conviction is not changed, though, by means of research, we find their sequential relation to be the result of the continuity of prior effects; we still retain the unaltered judgment, that, if we go back far enough, we must be in the presence of a cause. The mind cannot dispense with the link of power uniting sequences.

Then, if by long trains of sequential effects and secondary causes we are led up, not by demonstration, but by irresistible moral conviction, to a Primordial Power, a source of all, what is such creative cause? Is it inevitably God? Is the universe, as we know it, infinite? Who dare say?

Though we know that the vast looming firmament, in which the 'milky way' stretches its depths and winds its awful amplitudes, is beyond all finite power to follow; yet, it may be but a complex particle in a universe of universes, stretching on, and for ever on, over the bourneless immensity of the unknown.

If that be so, we can make no useful inference from our finite universe. We could infer only a finite creator from a finite cosmos. To be finite is to be infinitely less than infinite; and such a being could not be the ineffable majesty of mind and might, which we apprehend, but cannot comprehend, as the Creator.

If such a limited power could be conceived, because it is finite, it of necessity began to be; and therefore its very existence was of necessity caused. We seek *its* cause, as we do that of all other secondary causes; until at last we reach the only position in which there is mental rest, an infinite cause of all causes, the primordial and ultimate reality of all being.

Concerning even it, the question has arisen, Must not it also have been caused? Is not this question a paradox? It is of finite being only that we can affirm the necessity for causation. What is finite begins to be; what begins to be, must have been caused to be. But if our moral and reasoning faculties bring us at last, face to face, with an inscrutable and infinite primal cause, is there a mental process exercised by us that demands that such a being must have had a cause? Experiment cannot suggest it, for this is neither finite, nor a phenomenon; and can neither be observed nor analyzed; research in it is infinitely impossible; and of experience there can be none. Science is without function in presence of a primal cause. It is powerless, by virtue of its knowledge or its methods, to affirm or to deny an infinite and eternal self-existence. And yet such is not only possible to thought, but has congruity with all the faculties of reason. The principle of causality involves merely that every *finite* existence must have had a cause for its being; that what is born and dies, what arises and ceases to be, what began in time and flows on in continuous mutation, had an originator. But our consciousness of causality does not and cannot include or apply to an infinite and unsearchable cause of all. We may not with our finite plummet seek to measure the depths of the Infinite, nor with our limited grasp hope to enfold the All. To say nothing of its cause, what do we *know* of even the universe itself? We write and talk freely of millions of miles, and in a moment reverse the process and write or speak of millionths of a grain or of an inch; we think of tens of thousandths of a second, of millions of years, and duration that is without beginning and without end. Imagination cannot picture these things, though thought can possess them. They involve the two great mysteries ever present to mind, space and time.

Space includes within itself all that can be the subject of our knowledge, yet it is not a phenomenon, not an entity, not an object of sensation. It is a pure abstraction. No-space is not thinkable. By no effort of mind can we think of space as non-existent at any period in infinite duration. So far as we can see, without objects with their dimensional relations, space could not be a concept. The contents of space, out of which the mind abstracts space, are the source from whence our concept, space, emerges. An infinite void is mentally nothing; an intellect like man's, that had never realized extension in the dimensions of material bodies, could not present it in thought, any more than it can conceive correctly the qualities of a fourth dimension.

In like manner time is not a thing, an entity, to be accounted for as a creation, a thing caused; it is a consequence of existences; duration measured by sequences. If there were no succession of events, there would be no time. Space and time are mental abstractions, respectively, of the relations of dimensions and duration.

But with what mystery and majesty, with what proportions and powers, with what mass and movement is space full! and of what sequences and phenomena has time been the unconscious recorder! It is into these that the mind of man intently peers; it is across the bourneless area of uncharted space that he would carry his mental vision; it is into all the vicissitudes that have arisen, since the succession of cosmic phenomena marked off a section of duration, that the mind of man is ever struggling to thread its way; and if possible, to find the meaning and origin of it all.

That which is the most impressive outcome of all modern physical investigation, is the apparent mechanical automatism of all cosmic sequences and phenomena within our reach. As a result, the most powerful philosophies are directed to an endeavour to establish a mechanical—that is, a mindless or purposeless—*origin* of the universe. But granted a universe, fully understood, exhaustively known, purely mechanical in all its *present* activities; even this, surely, only makes more absolute the certainty that the very conditions of its present existence, involved at its beginning, a more majestic design than all the thinkers of the past had ever dreamed.

There is no alternative; either chance, or mental purpose, gave primal origin to all that is. Nothing within the reach of intellect could express the infinite improbability of the first suggestion. That *one* vast harmony, one *perfect* method, should fall out by chance, through the operation of uncounted millenniums of ages, is almost inexpressibly improbable; but that a system of harmonies, practically infinite in number and measureless in extent, should all be locked together in one vast uniting harmony, making all creation a chorus, to which all its parts from the centre to the margin contribute their flowing and concerted strains, without a discord to the unity of thought; to say that *that* arose by chance, sprang from fortuity, fell out by accident, is surely to trifle with the fundamental principles of our moral faculties and reasoning powers.

Hence, nothing but philosophical ruin can be the end of materialism when enunciated in its grosser form. But our age is distinguished by the existence of a brilliant philosophical materialism, which has arrested, and is swaying, the deepest thought of our age, by the opulence of its learning and resource, by the scientific accuracy and insight of its abounding and perfect illustrations, and by the subtile, but stately method and breadth of its generalizations; but beyond all, by the fact that its world-famed author, Mr. Herbert Spencer, repels, with warmth, persistence, and manifest integrity, the very suspicion of 'materialism'!

Yet we are compelled to ask, of what value, of what real service, are all the ideal and spiritual assumptions of his splendid and fascinating philosophy? It acknowledges a *something* beyond the matter and the mechanism that fills the amplitudes of space; it even designates this something a 'power.' But that power is declared, for ever and infinitely, beyond the circumference of knowledge: it is the 'absolute,' the 'unknowable;' it can take no part, and become no agent in, no factor of, any philosophy of the origin of the universe which we construct. On the very terms of the philosophy itself, all in heaven and earth, through all the past and all the future, can be accounted for and explained without it. If the admission into its phraseology of the existence of a 'power,' which is a name only, be taken as sufficient reason, then this philosophy is not materialistic. But if it be remembered that this 'power' is absolutely without function in this philosophy of the construction of the universe,—if it be true to its formula,—and that only matter and motion are asked for, its ultimate materialism is a certainty, and, from its very subtilty, a peril.

To philosophical Theism the coarser Materialism can bring no lasting danger. It ignores too much, and assumes too much; and treats with a too manifest disdain the fundamental basis of our reasoning faculties.

It has many brilliant exponents; but foremost amongst them is Haeckel of Jena, a man of large scientific attainments, a biologist of the highest repute, and possessed of the keenest acumen. But these are not the only, nor the essential factors, of a philosophic mind.

He has no hesitancy, no scruple. A Creator for him is

a conception for scorn, and he pours unceasing contempt upon the thought that he or any of us are more than material organisms, alive for our little day and then dead for ever. There is a future only for the race. The universe is declared to be without purpose; it is moving matter, which, by self-operation through immeasurable duration, has issued in laws that exist without reason, and devoid of an originator, act, with the deafness of the rock and the unconsciousness of the sea; producing in the realm of life the weaker and the stronger, but only for that unceasing war in which the stronger win.

That for man there is nothing nobler, nothing higher, than to study the grinding laws which compel him; which laws are the summaries of natural methods which began in nothing, and have been for ever vacant of thought or purpose.

We need have no anxiety concerning the influence of such a scheme; from its own incoherence it enfolds its intellectual death-warrant in its very form.

But the philosophy of Spencer is of another order. It is a philosophy that scorns the idealism of Berkeley, and that with the fervour of conviction, indignantly repudiates 'Materialism.' He contends for the equal and independent reality of self and not-self, of subject and object, of mind and matter. He affirms that the 'co-existence of subject and object is a deliverance of consciousness . . . and is a truth transcending all others in certainty.'[1] Yet, in the progress of the philosophy, we discover that from matter in motion, and nothing else, the whole universe is supposed to arise; life emerges; and mind, in its most transcendent

[1] *Principles of Psychology*, vol. i. p. 209.

forms comes forth. And it is this fallacy pervading the philosophy that is the essence of its power. Repudiating 'Materialism' as philosophically untenable, it yet exists as a philosophy to endeavour to show that mind is an outcome of matter.

Look at the problem it sets for solution. 'Philosophy,' says Spencer, 'is *completely unified* knowledge;' and adds, '... a philosophy stands self-convicted of inadequacy, if it does not formulate the whole series of changes passed through by every existence. ... If it begins its explanations with existences that already have concrete forms ... then manifestly they had preceding histories ... of which no account is given. And as such preceding ... histories are subjects of possible knowledge, a philosophy which says nothing about them falls short of the required unification.'[1]

Then, on the very terms of the philosophy, we are to contemplate 'the beginning' with absolutely nothing anterior or unaccounted for. There must be no 'concrete forms,' no 'preceding histories,' to be encountered.

Now observe, it is clearly recognised in this philosophy that the ultimate nature of all that constitutes the universe is infinitely beyond the reach of the human mind; that in their final nature time, space, matter, motion, rest, the transfer of motion, the exercise of force, the nature and operation of consciousness and thought, are all equally, that is, infinitely, inscrutable. Knowledge is inexorably limited to, and co-extensive with, phenomena; yet from these phenomena alone we are to obtain exhaustive accounts of their own origin and existence, in spite of the admitted inscrutable mysteries of which they are the manifestations.

[1] *First Principles*, pp. 541–42.

If we can obtain so complete a knowledge of matter and motion, by a scientific study of them, as will enable us, with that knowledge alone, to explain their origin and account for the sequences they involve, then there is no more mystery. There are no 'ultimates' to explain. Our knowledge covers all that is, in space and time. The 'Absolute' itself is a meaningless superfluity, and the mysterious 'power' that is philosophically invoked can have no true place, for all is explicable without it.

A beginning is inevitable to a philosophy of material evolution. Then 'in the beginning' what? How in the zero, in which there were no 'concrete forms' and no 'preceding histories,' did the first movement towards the plenished arch of heaven and the fruitful earth arise? Concentration and diffusion, it is affirmed, are universally observed physical processes. The latest 'science in tracing back the genealogies of various objects finds' that 'their components were once in diffused states, and, pursuing their histories forwards, finds diffused states will be again assumed by them.'[1] Clearly, then, 'matter' is assumed to exist at the 'beginning.' It certainly *may* have had a 'preceding history;' and to ignore this is to come, at the outset, perilously near to a philosophy 'that stands self-convicted of inadequacy.'

A diffused state of matter is, it thus appears, the earliest point of the beginning that physical evolution can descry. This is the nebular hypothesis of Laplace; without doubt a majestic theory, but a theory still. Science has welcomed it to work with; and it explains, or aids in the interpretation of, much; but, that it should be taken so for granted as

[1] *First Principles*, p. 280.

to be considered a demonstrated or even undisputed and established fact of modern science, we may be permitted to doubt; and it must have had a 'preceding history.' It takes us to a point in measureless past duration, where all that is now concrete matter is assumed to have been in a gaseous state. It is not even contended that it is an original condition. Such an almost infinite mass of nebulous matter must have been due, if existent, to heat, and to heat of an intensity that defies our range of conception.

But whence did such heat come? 'Heat' is demonstrated to us now as a rhythmic 'mode of motion;' one of the phenomena of nature to be accounted for. Verily, heat is a phenomenon with a 'preceding history,' and yet at the outset its presence is assumed in the cosmic cloud.

But, further complexity still, how does heat act in this primordial nebula? If heat is a 'mode of motion,' by what were the heat vibrations wrought? You must have *then*, for the phenomenon of heat, what is indispensable to the physical theory of it now :—the inconceivable but indispensable ether of modern physics. But how came the ether in, and beyond, the cosmic cloud? It is an 'existence,' manifestly; more, it is 'matter;' but matter that transcends the range of the action of gravity; it is without weight, and differentiated from all matter that we know in a manner that thought cannot follow.

How did this 'existence' pass from the imperceptible to the perceptible? and by its own requirement should not a complete philosophy furnish its past history?

Let us come more closely into contact with the actual formula of this philosophy. 'Evolution,' says Spencer, 'is an integration of matter and concomitant dissipation of motion, during which the matter passes from an indefinite, incoherent homogeneity to a definite, coherent heterogeneity, and during which the retained motion undergoes a parallel transformation.'[1]

Here, then, are the factors of the potential universe. By definition they are the sole structural essentials. Beyond them nothing should be asked, required, or assumed. What are these irreducible factors of the formula? 'Matter' and 'motion.' But we have clearly seen that we are cognizant of matter as such only by its 'modes of motion.' It is *these* for which evolution has to account. 'Matter' denuded of the qualities by which we now are cognizant of it, can be no other than dimensions without qualities, spatial presence undiscoverable by sense.

On the other hand, pure motion, motion by itself, is impossible to thought. Motion is only known as an affection of matter. 'It becomes manifest,' says Spencer, 'that our experience of *force* is that out of which our idea of matter is built.'[2] But, in the terms of the formula, force can be nothing but matter affected by motion. What, then, was this primary matter on which motion first acted, and before motion had by various 'modes' produced in it a single quality? No answer is possible; but, nevertheless, as the philosophy unfolds itself we find that 'we need not refrain . . . from dealing with matter as made up of extended and resistant atoms,'[3] and henceforth we are led to consider the cosmic nebula as not only homogeneous, but as being, in its homogeneity, atomic.

[1] *First Principles*, p. 396.   [2] *First Principles*, p. 167.
[3] *First Principles*, p. 176.

No lover of physical and chemical science can do other than profoundly admire the atomic theory of modern physics. But there is no sound physicist or chemist but is sufficiently alive to its difficulties to know that in every form in which it has been presented, it is, to say no more, tentative and hypothetic. In Mr. Spencer's philosophy it becomes a fundamental fact of the beginning. But the existence of atoms being granted, how did they arise? 'If you ask the materialist,' says Professor Tyndall, 'whence is this matter . . . who or what divided it into molecules . . . he has no answer.'[1] So that here, in spite of the claim made, no philosophy can be 'complete;' and even the doctrine of an eternally automatic evolution is philosophically inadequate.

But these atoms of the primordial haze are 'resistant;' such a quality can only result from a special affection of matter by motion; whence came or how arose such an affection of matter? Its existence in the atoms of the nebula inevitably implies 'preceding history,' but it is not given; and this pregnant atomic haze is, so far as we can see, without colour, without chemical affinity or reaction, without light, electricity, or magnetism, and devoid of all cohesion.

Clearly, these are not the atoms of the chemical elements known to us. They are not the atoms of Dalton nor of Clark Maxwell. The atoms of the cosmic mist are, by the very terms of the formula, naked of quality; and, by the limiting conditions of the definition of the cloud as homogeneous, are, throughout all the abysms of space, alike in size, in shape, and in motions. Equal extensions of space moving at equal rates.

[1] *Fragments of Science,* vol. ii. p. 396.

By these conditions, then, it is manifest that primordial matter is in itself infinitely powerless and inert. Motion can affect it; but can there be motion of any *new* kind originated without a power to cause it? If that can be, the fundamental acts of human reason are untrustworthy; and man is incapable of knowledge or deduction, which is absurd. Then what was the power that determined new motions in the primordial homogeneous matter?

It could not by any demand in the formula be even gravity, if that were competent. Modern thought and knowledge cannot allow gravitation to be a property of matter. Ether is matter, but it does not gravitate. Gravity is therefore an occult affection of matter by motion, that has a history 'to be accounted for.'

In this almost infinite primal nebula, a certain class of motion is assumed. How it originated is unexplained. But what is the atomic motion of this primal homogeneous matter? From the terms given it must be as I have said. Motion of absolute likeness throughout all the profounds of space it filled; equalized motion in every atom; no difference of rate; no difference of mode. The motion of one atom is identic with the motion of all. It could never be lost; it could never increase; it could never alter. It is homogeneous, and *therefore* changeless—balanced for ever—in itself. Says Mr. Spencer: 'Any finite mass of diffused matter, even though vast enough to form our whole sidereal system,' if it were of 'absolute sphericity, absolute uniformity of composition, and absolute symmetry of relation to all forces external to it,'[1] would be homogeneous and eternally incapable of change.

[1] *First Principles*, p. 407.

And that 'homogeneity' is the very condition laid down for the beginning, from which mechanical evolution is to educe the universe. In the Spencerian formula there is no qualification of the term homogeneous. It postulates 'an indefinite, incoherent homogeneity,' that is, an indefinite cloud, with balanced motion in all its atoms which neither attracts nor repels, and is in itself infinitely incapable of change.

Now, shall we not ask *how* the first pulse, that caused the stupendously vast homogeneity to throb into the heterogeneous, arose? whence did it come? Infinite incapacity could not, unless reason be mendacious, render *itself* capable. Then how came that *first* movement that, it is argued, ended in revolving systems, a bountiful earth, the throat of the nightingale, and the tragedy of Macbeth!

There is no answer. This philosophy, to get the first progressive movement in its balanced nebula, bids its formula stand aside, that it may advance. At a critical moment it changes the very meaning of the homogeneous. 'The condition of homogeneity is a condition of unstable equilibrium!'[1] 'The phrase . . . . . is one used in mechanics to express a balance of forces of such kind that the interference of any further force, however minute, will destroy the arrangement previously subsisting, and bring about a totally different arrangement.'[2]

Note, then, the homogeneous cosmic cloud is, by the terms given, in equilibrium. But some 'further force,' some small influence *outside* itself, acts upon it, and it breaks up.

But what is the *outside* influence? What is this 'further

[1] *First Principles*, p. 401.   [2] *Ibid.* p. 401–402.

know of the Method of Creation. 27

force,' and from whence? We have a cloud composed of atoms in balanced motion—nothing more. Outside influence, 'further force,' is an intrusion. It has no right there. It has not on the wedding garment of the formula.

Surely an outside influence must be caused? If it involved no more energy than is wielded by a may-fly's wing, how came it there? It is as easy to admit the *self-origination* of a divinity of power, as the *self-creation* of power to lift a grain. It is not in the philosophy; 'outside influence' has no credentials, and the admission of inability to evolve the universe without it, is an admission that the mechanical philosophy fails at the outset. Nor can it serve the emergency to invoke 'force.'

A Divine origin of the universe is usually rejected, because the Divinity eludes the methods of science. But we cannot supplant the Deity by enthroning force. Science can tell us what force *does*, but it can no more find what force *is*, than what an infinite mind is. Force is an irresistible mental inference from matter in motion, but its ultimate nature is defiantly beyond the reach of science.

It appears, then, that to obtain even the 'elements' of our modern chemistry, the philosophy of mechanical evolution must, at the beginning, call in uncovenanted aid. Let us remember this, while for the purposes of argument we allow it. There may have been secured, added, and perhaps altered, motion by the surreptitious 'outside influence;' but it can be nothing more. The atoms are still without property, and are only affected by motion. Have we any *experience* to induce us to believe that atoms without property, even affected by thermal vibrations and pushed by gravity, will build themselves up into the seventy 'elements' of chemistry with their specific and inalienable qualities? That, through vibrations of heat and pushings of gravity, they could become hydrogen and mercury, carbon and gold, chlorine and phosphorus! And these properties being thus acquired, by their sheer interactions that all the chemistry, the physics, and the *order* of all the area of space within the galaxy arose? This is what the formula of the most brilliant philosophy of any age would lead us to infer.

In this relation I do not forget the recent and splendid service done by Mr. Crooks to the philosophical side of chemistry in the record of his researches on 'The Genesis of the Elements.' It is a most subtile and exquisite means of endeavouring to deduce the *method*, the '*law*' according to which what we know as the 'chemical elements' were built up. He obtains indications of a primitive element— a something out of which the elements were evolved. He calls it *protyle* or first stuff, and from its presence he concludes that the elements, as we know them, 'are not simple and primordial, that they have not arisen by chance, or been created in a desultory and mechanical manner, but have been evolved from simpler matter—or perhaps indeed from one sole kind of matter.'[1]

But this reduction of matter, as we know it, to a simpler but still highly differentiated condition, only causes reason the more earnestly to demand how, the rhythmic and complex method, which we express by the word 'law,' came into operation, and was established for ever.

The 'protyle' is infinitely more complex than the atoms of the homogeneous nebula. It makes no philoso-

[1] Reprint of a Lecture at the Royal Institution by Mr. Crooks, p. 2.

phical difference whether the ultimate atoms of the bodies known as elementary are all alike, or in each instance special. In either case there is infinitely more in the matter they severally make, than can be deduced from motion affecting the primitive atoms.

But not only have we by the formula and constructive method of this philosophy to obtain protyle from the mere effects of motion on primitive atoms; but, by the same means alone, we have to change protyle into the seventy 'elements;' above all, without an added factor or a change in the method, we have to rise to life!

Let us reflect. By life in this relation is meant that which lives, an organism endowed with life's properties. Are these properties unique? Or is there some point of fluxion where the properties of life at their minima arise in the activities of not-life at some undiscovered maxima? A point at which some occult molecular complexities arise, changing matter dead into matter living?

The answer must come, not through our abstract logic, but from our laboratories.

Life, it is well known, has its phenomena inherent in, and strictly confined to, a highly complex compound, with fixed chemical constituents. This compound, in its living state, is known as protoplasm. It is clear, colourless, and, to our finest optical resources, devoid of discoverable structure. There is not a living thing on earth but possesses its life in protoplasm, from a microscopic fungus to man.

To depict the properties of life in irreducible simplicity, take one of the lowliest instances within the present range of science. Let it be one of the exquisitely minute, almost infinitely prolific, and universally diffused living forms that set up and carry on putrefaction. The lesser of them may, when considered as solid specks, vary from the fifty thousand millionth of a cubic inch to the twenty billionth of a cubic inch. I select one that is oval in shape. It moves with the agility of the grayling and the grace of a swallow, the motion resulting from the rhythmic action of two motile fibres.

This free and self-originating action is its first vital quality.

Its mission as an organism, is to break up and set free the chemical elements that had been locked up in dead organic compounds. Its own substance wears out by this and other means; and it has the power to renovate the waste from the dead decomposition in which it lives; constructing, in the laboratory of its protoplasm, new living matter.

This is the second characteristic of that alone which lives. By it, living matter is *sui generis*. Every instant, and at the same temperature, this inconceivably minute speck, without discoverable structure, effects analyses and complicated syntheses which either baffle all the synthetic chemistry of man, or else, where he is able to accomplish the simplest of the organic syntheses, it is by processes and at temperatures that make all life impossible.

But more, this vital and inconceivably minute speck multiplies with astounding rapidity in two ways; by the first and common process, in the course of a minute and a half the entire body is divided into two precisely similar bodies, each one being perfect; almost immediately these again divide, and so on in geometric ratio through all the populated fluid; the rapidity of this intense and wonderful vital action transcending all thought. By this process alone a single form may in three hours give rise to a population of organisms as great as the human population of the globe.

But this is not all; at certain stages of the organism self-division ceases. The final divisions result in strikingly modified forms of the organism; these approach each other and melt together. They are then shining globules without action, but at the end of a given time they open, and pour out a continuous cloud of minutest spore or ova, which are as countless as the sands; and from these arise again another host of the organisms, which pass again through all the mystery and marvel of this vital cycle.

And this is the third of the qualities that make what lives absolutely unique amidst the things of earth.

This is life—whether vegetable or animal none can determine—in the simplest form in which it can be known; life that is possessed only of the irreducible properties which are inalienable, and which distinguish it for ever and everywhere from what is not-life.

It is true that the philosopher, by the common consent of mind, occupies the throne of intellect; but it is not, for all that, to the esoteric philosopher, not to the deep mental seer, who girdles all space, all duration, all phenomena with his thought, that nature reveals her latest, her subtlest, her profoundest secrets. It is to the patient student—nature's loving learner, whose eye and ear are trained to read her faintest writing and catch her lowest whisper—that her deepest truths in all their strength and immediate bearing are disclosed. Yet the fates of philosophies are determined by these.

Then what is the testimony of students and searchers as to the mode in which life takes its origin to-day? Does life originate *in* life? or do we find that in our laboratories, and in the observed processes of nature *now*, the not-living can be, without the intervention of living things, changed into that which lives?

Biology, as a science, answers 'no.' Says the greatest master of all the facts, Professor Huxley: 'The properties of living matter distinguish it absolutely from all other kinds of things, and,' he continues, 'the present state of our knowledge furnishes us with no link between the living and the not-living.'[1]

Then what lives is, in its qualities, utterly unlike — sharply marked off from — what is not living. Yet the elements that make up the living stuff are the most common on the earth. Carbon, hydrogen, oxygen, nitrogen: we know them each and all; we know their properties and reactions on each other, and on all the minor elements of the living matter; but that knowledge only complicates the nature of the problem. The mystery of life is, not that any occult elements compose the matter in which it dwells; the mystery of life consists solely in the question, *how* the elements that make up protoplasm can be so combined, as, by their combination, to acquire the splendid and solitary properties of that which lives.

Manifestly, then, there was a time in the past history of the globe, when its matter was without life, and therefore there must have been a time, perhaps at a point of intense activity in the not-living matter of the globe, when it became endowed with the properties of life.

[1] *Ency. Brit.* art. 'Biology,' vol. iii. p. 679.

By what agency that transcendent upward movement was wrought, science claims no vocation to inquire. But let the earth, and air, and sea, with all their teeming denizens, attest,—that power was competent.

Now let us ask, can we as rational beings account for all the properties of living things in terms of matter and motion? Will vibrating atoms, with millenniums of ages to work in, but no power to direct them, explain the wonder? Was the transmutation of not-living matter into living brought about merely by what we can reduce to solid geometry and transcendental numbers? atoms, which we can approximately measure, dancing to the rhythm of complex motion?

All that mechanical evolution has to work with, is atoms and motions. Pile the atoms into complexities too large for clear thought, cluster molecule round molecule, and let them beat in multitudinous harmonies defiant of conception, yet all you have is matter in motion. It is not life with its sentiency; it is not life with its self-chosen movement; it is not life with its power to construct its own substance out of matter that is dead, and to multiply its kind *ad libitum.*

And yet Mr. Spencer begins by taking what no mental manipulation of the naked formula of his philosophy could provide, the 'elements' of our present chemistry; and by imagining higher and higher complexities of atomic structure a complicated molecule is reached; and then, by a change in name, which is justified by no change in the facts, he calls the complex substance organic matter; and by simply continuing this process, thinks he sees it become living.[1]

[1] *Principles of Biology,* vol. i. p. 481.

The justification of all this is the affirmation 'that organic matter was not produced all at once,' and that there is in the laboratory of the chemist 'what we may literally call artificial evolution.' Mr. Spencer instances a laboratory product of what is counted a sufficiently typical organic compound.[1] But to obtain it the chemist has to employ no less than twenty distinct chemical and physical processes, involving many varying temperatures, from a red heat to the intensity of the electric arc, and between thirty and forty reagents and their products, are employed in the process. Compare this with the silent and impenetrable simplicity of the chemistry of life, and vivid and striking is the contrast. And yet when this product of the chemist lies before you, produced by the tremendous relative labours of the laboratory, it is as far off from dead white of egg, to say nothing of living protoplasm, as the qualities of a flint pebble are from the qualities of the diamond.

The *facts* of nature—surely our safest guide—declare that the transition from not-life to life is abrupt. The break is absolute and clear. A 'complex molecule' is a molecule of atoms in motion,—nothing more. More atoms and more motion cannot, by themselves, as Mr. Spencer would teach, make it 'organic;' much less can any further addition of atoms and tremors make it live. It is in vain for Haeckel to call the simplest moneron that lives 'primeval slime,' or to call numbers of them 'individualized lumps of albumen.' It is a travesty. Under the same lens place 'a lump of albumen' and the lowest *living* infusorian, and a voiceless contradiction of Haeckel's phrase which none can ever question is indubitably given. The infusorian

[1] The Butyrate of dimethylamin.

lives; the albumen is dead. The infusorian constructs the vital matter of its own body from the heterogeneous matter in which it lives; the albumen decomposes as it lies there. The infusorian has soon multiplied by millions, while the albumen disappears by decadence. To write of living monera as 'albumen,' or of 'complex molecules' with nothing more than their complexity, as *living*, is to contradict, in the name, the essential and distinguishing qualities of both.

This impropriety may be yet more manifest by another quotation from Haeckel. His aim is to endeavour by the use of vague language to reduce the impassable gulf between the living and the not-living, and he writes of the animal *ovum* as 'a little lump of albumen in which another albuminous body is enclosed—the nucleus.' What profound trifling is this! Think of, say a human ovum, an invisible particle less than the hundredth of an inch in diameter; it *lives;* and there lies coiled up in the mystery of its minuteness all the potentiality of the highest manhood; all the possible power of Socrates, or Homer, or Goethe. Is that simply 'a lump of albumen'? Not unless a man can be justly described as such, by the bottles of chemical substances to which his body can be reduced.

Even Mr. Spencer pleads that 'the lowest living things are not, properly speaking, organisms at all, for they have no distinctions of parts, no traces of organization.' If it were true that our lenses cannot reveal organization in the lowliest and smallest organisms, does it follow that there *is* none? Will Mr. Spencer risk the validity of the doctrine of material atoms on the ability of our lenses to show the atom? Surely not.

But the affirmation is not supported by facts. The splendid increase of microscopical lens power during the past decade has not only enabled us to see that there is complexity and structure in both the animal and vegetable cell, which bisects by an elaborate process; but even the minute nucleus of the minutest organisms, often not more than one tenth part of the infinitesimal body itself, is now proved to undergo profound structural changes, which precede all the great cyclic changes of the organism as a whole. The nucleus is the centre, in fact, of all the higher activities of the least and lowest infusoria; and is the centre of most delicate but clearly demonstrable structural changes.[1]

We cannot reduce the mystery of life by treating contemptuously its ultimate cells. They are as defiant of interpretation by our present methods as the more complex structures they compose. The mystery of life, *per se*, is as great and as deep, in a monad and a mildew, as in a man. Every attempt to argue away the meaning of vital function and property, on the basis of the organic simplicity of unicellular organisms, is wholly fallacious. It is knowledge, not speculation, which affirms that the least and lowest, as well as the largest and most complex of living forms, are 'distinguished absolutely from all other kinds of things. There is 'no link' between matter living and matter without life. To attempt to build up 'life' by slow increments of added complexity, in atomic or molecular structure, is a philosophical ingenuity; but it expresses no natural truth within the horizon of our knowledge. A higher number of primal, or even chemical atoms, arranged in the most

[1] *Jour. Roy. Micro. Soc.*, President's Address, 1886.

complex ratios, and affected by the most rhythmic movements, are not the data from which to deduce a living organism. And to affirm of the lowest living things that 'they are not, properly speaking, organisms at all,'[1] because the instruments used at a given date did not reveal structure, is, at best, an *argumentum a silentio;* while simultaneously it contradicts the facts of biology, and assumes the whole point at issue.

On the other hand, there is not a single fact within the present range of our knowledge that indicates, or even suggests, that the quarternary compounds approximate, under any known conditions, to the state of matter living.

As the sheets of this Lecture are passing through the press, Sir Henry Roscoe, as President of the British Association, has delivered a brilliant and essentially scientific address. On the subject of chemistry none can speak with a voice more authoritative: and on this very question he writes as follows: 'But now the question may well be put—Is any limit set to this synthetic power of the chemist? Although the danger of dogmatizing as to the progress of science has already been shown in too many instances, yet one cannot help feeling that the barrier which exists between the organized and unorganized worlds is one which the chemist sees no chance of breaking down. It is true that there are those who profess to foresee that the day will arrive, when the chemist, by a succession of constructive efforts, may pass beyond albumen, and gather the elements of lifeless matter into a living structure. Whatever may be said regarding this from other standpoints, the chemist can only say that at present no such

[1] *Principles of Biology*, vol. i. p. 482.

problem lies within his province. Protoplasm, with which the simplest manifestations of life are associated, is not a compound, but a structure built up of compounds. The chemist may successfully synthesize any of its component molecules, but he has no more reason to look forward to the synthetic production of the structure than to imagine that the synthesis of gallic acid leads to the artificial production of gall-nuts.'[1]

To assume, then, that by starting with atoms in equilibriated motions, uncounted millenniums of ages ago, and that by adding atoms and groups of atoms, with altered and re-altered motions as the ages roll away, with the result that at last, with these factors and no others, we shall get organism and life, is, surely, as fallacious as to explain Millais's picture of the Huguenots as having been brought about by a skilful arrangement of palettes and brushes, easels and pigments.

Now let it be clearly recalled that Charles Darwin involved himself in none of this philosophic ambiguity. To him life was more than a complexity of elementary atoms affected by motion. It was something he could not 'explain.' He postulated, therefore, the unexplained presence of 'primordial living germs,' endowed with the properties, which, experience teaches, are possessed by living matter to-day.

How, in the great past, mineral and gaseous matters on this earth were, as a question of scientific method, so affected as to become living matter is, to our present resources at least, impenetrable.

---

[1] The *Times* report of the address of Sir H. E. Roscoe before the British Association at Manchester.—*Times*, September 1, 1887.

> 'Flower in the crannied wall,
> I pluck you out of the crannies;
> I hold you here, root and all, in my hand,
> Little flower.—But *if* I could understand
> What you are, root and all, and all in all,
> I should know what God and man is.'

I merely contend that whatever were the means by which dead matter first lived, they were higher, infinitely higher, than matter and motion; they could only have been the resources of a *competent* power.

I adopt gladly the language of Professor Huxley: 'Belief, in the scientific sense of the word,' he says, 'is a serious matter, and needs strong foundations. To say, therefore, in the admitted absence of evidence, that I have any belief as to the mode in which existing forms of life have originated, would be using words in a wrong sense. But expectation is permissible where belief is not; and if it were given me to look beyond the abyss of geologically recorded time to the still more remote period when the earth was passing through physical and chemical conditions, which it can no more see again than a man can recall his infancy, I should expect to be a witness of the evolution of living protoplasm from not-living matter.'[1] So should I.

By what other means than by the operation of natural 'laws' can we think of the Infinite Power, extending through all extent, as the fountain of all being, as acting? Every process of nature that ever man has investigated throughout all space and all time, results from a perfect and unalterable method which we call a 'law' of nature. Then why should the primal process, by which not-living matter became, once for all, living, be brought about by any other

[1] *Critiques and Addresses*, p. 239.

means than the predetermined action of competent natural laws? Because life—living matter—does not *now* arise directly from that which is not-life, does it follow that the creative method was discontinuous? that the primordial creative laws willed into operation 'in the beginning' were only competent to evolve the inorganic and not-living? and that at this point a supernatural 'interference,' a 'miraculous interposition,' had to be effected to endow what was dead with the transcendent properties of life? The whole line of human experience, interpreted in the light of modern scientific knowledge, compels the conclusion that the 'primordial germs' in which life on earth began, arose by the operation of natural creative laws. That an energy, not now operating within the area of our experience, was at work, when not-living matter progressed into living structure, is certain. But there is nothing, within the range of our knowledge, that permits the inference that it was brought about by any other means, than such as, if we could have seen them in operation, we should have called 'laws' of nature. This view surely ennobles without limit our fatally humanized view of creative action. 'The beginning' was thus, by the unsearchable mystery of a creative mind and will, the *potentiality* of all the universe through all its duration; which it only required 'time' in which the potential powers and modes should operate, to make actual, in the universe we see.

As the highest mental powers and products of the most gifted of our race, were originally potential in the primitive ovum from which each took his origin, so, it is congruous, and capable of being grasped by our thought although it cannot be portrayed by our imagination, that the mind and will of the inscrutable Creator prevised and preordered the whole series of conditions which, by their immutable action, interaction, and rhythmic concurrence as 'laws,' evolved the universe.

So far as the finest and keenest researches in chemistry and physics carry us, especially such researches as those of Crooks and Lockyer, it is powerfully indicated that the creative method in the inorganic world was a sublime progressive plan, a building up by law, of the dome of heaven and the floor of earth, and all that goes with both. But behind the matter and the motion, above the energies and the force, there surely was, as we have been constrained to see, what we can only think of as the conception, the purpose, and the will by which the evolving order, marked in high, and higher sublimity, the upward and onward movement of the ripening and uncounted ages.

But when the highest point of the inorganic, the not-living, was reached, and a new factor had to appear in the world to crown some of its matter with *life* and all its wonders, what was it that ensued? If 'law' did not cease to act; if there were no break in the continuity of evolution, and yet a factor of power, not now operating within the range of our knowledge, was absolutely necessary to change the not-living matter of the earth into matter that lived, how was it brought about?

Our inability to reply, does not invalidate the facts on the one hand, nor justify attempts at explanations that find no sanction in experience and knowledge on the other.

Suggestion by analogy, feeble as it is, is the nearest approach that we can make to the solution of what must, perhaps, remain for ever a splendid mystery.

If creation be, then, the expression of the mind and will of a Creator, uttered in method and issuing in phenomena, he must see the end from the beginning: his resource is infinite. The human mathematician, of the highest order, can devise, with all the adaptations and prearrangements that are needed, an instrument or machine, which shall continue for a number of motions, without necessary limit, according to a primal law, but which by such prevised and preordered arrangements would, suddenly, at the required point of time, undergo change, and operate henceforth after a law entirely new.

An instrument has actually been made which was competent to effect the solution of quadratic equations whose roots are real. One has also been made capable of effecting the determination of the real roots of any equation. It is perfectly conceivable that an instrument could be made which should go on finding the real roots only, for a measured time, and then by a prearranged and provided method should suddenly, by the very laws and principles of its construction, so change, that for another period, or for evermore, it should also determine the imaginary roots.

Is it not conceivable that infinite resource, infinite wisdom, infinite prevision and power could in a manner which this illustration only suggests have caused the non-vital universe to become in some parts vital? Could not infinite power, infinite wisdom, the originator of all that we call material phenomena, have prevised and preordered, in the impenetrable mystery of 'the beginning,' that the creative laws of evolution for an inorganic world, should, as they brought about the completion of their perfect purpose, have carried with them from that 'beginning' preordered potentialities, that should, by the primal volition of the Creator, emerge, as an inevitable and orderly sequence, into the operation of higher activities and new laws?

If that may not be, it is not a divine being that is in our thought. But if that may be, then the self-acting laws of nature are self-acting, as the products of eternal mind and will. Each self-acting phenomenon is, to us, an embodied thought of God; emerging in matter now, as a consequence of the sublimity and perfection of the methods divinely willed 'in the beginning.'

Let this illustration weigh for what it will; this at least is clear, that the mechanical philosophy, whether or not it refuses to be called 'material,' has proved its formula incompetent. Atomic matter without property, affected by motion, with persistent relations between the matter and the motion, can no more account for the universe even up to the point of the origin of the lowest life, than the vibrations of a musical chord can account for the joy begotten of music.

But how stands the problem of its origin, when, in that which lives, we include the presence of mind? None more firmly contends for the absolute disparity, the entire and unqualified difference between mind and matter, than Mr. Spencer. To him there can be nothing within the whole realm of thought severed by a wider interval than consciousness and thought on the one hand, and matter on the other. 'Just,' he says, 'in the same way that the object is the unknown permanent *nexus* which is never itself a phenomenon, but is that which holds phenomena together, so is the subject the unknown permanent *nexus* which is never itself a state of consciousness, but which holds all states of consciousness together.'[1] Mind and matter, then, are here admitted to be infinitely unlike, but absolutely equal realities. This is boldly reaffirmed; he says: 'No effort of imagination enables us to think of a shock, however minute, except as undergone by an entity. We are compelled, therefore, to postulate a substance of mind that is affected, before we can think of its affections.'[2]

This is as clear as a geometric definition. Mind and matter are admitted to be the two opposite termini of thought; they are divided by an interval beyond which thought cannot go. They are symbolized as x and y, two equally unknown, but absolutely unlike, quantities. Beyond the common fact of existence, there is not a quality of the one that is not infinitely unlike all the qualities of the other.

What this disparity is we all know: enough, that matter is inert, absolutely without perceiving power, and unable in itself to move or to produce motion. But mind is conscious, knows that it exists; and, however mysteriously, originates motion. Matter has mass; mind is absolutely without it. Matter cannot be thought of save as an occupant of space. Mind has no extension.

Is it conceivable, then, that we should be required by this philosophy, which thus admits the utter disparity of mind and matter, to make mind a function of matter? that we should be asked to mentally follow a process by which y shall be changed into x? This verily is so!

I must repeat the formula of this philosophy of evolution. 'Evolution is an integration of matter, and concomitant dissipation of motion, during which the matter

[1] *Principles of Psychology,* vol. ii. p. 484.   [2] *Ibid.* vol. i. p. 627.

passes from an indefinite, incoherent homogeneity to a definite, coherent heterogeneity, and during which the retained motion undergoes a parallel transformation.'

Matter and motion, these are the all; no suggestion of aught besides. Then, if on that formula the philosophy is built, the rhythmic vicissitudes through which matter has passed during limitless millenniums of time, are supposed to be able to change matter's unconsciousness into self-perception and thought; to cause extended and gravitating mass to pass into an unextended realization of its own being, unyoked to gravity; to emerge from space relations involving motion produced by outside forces, to an absolute independence of space relations which makes motion impossible. If we make our *knowledge* of phenomena and the processes and methods of Nature the basis of our judgment, is it not manifest, that such a change is incapable of being thought?

The unknown y, that is, matter, must, by sheer physical vicissitudes, actually abnegate its own qualities, and emerge, no longer *itself*, y, but another entity, infinitely unlike itself, that is, x!

If mind and matter are divergent from each other by infinite unlikeness of quality, the mind refuses assent, that any process, based on the foundation of accurate human knowledge, would sanction the emergence of mind by physical processes from matter. Mind is the antithesis, and cannot be a function, of matter.

The mind is intimately linked with cerebral action. We do not know mind apart from brain; but there is no discovered correlation between the *work* of the brain, and consciousness. Dr. Tyndall, whose keen and instructed intellect has addressed itself to this deep problem from the position of a physicist, says, amongst many similar utterances: 'But when we endeavour to pass . . . from the phenomena of physics to those of thought, we meet a problem which transcends any conceivable expansion of the powers which we now possess. We may think over the subject again and again, but it eludes all intellectual presentation. We stand at length face to face with the incomprehensible. The territory of physics is wide, but it has its limits, from which we look with vacant gaze into the region beyond, . . . and thus it will ever loom, compelling the philosophies of successive ages to confess that—

> "We are such stuff
> As dreams are made of, and our life
> Is rounded by a sleep."' [1]

The same thinker asks, 'What is the causal connexion . . . between molecular motions and states of consciousness?' And he answers that neither he nor any other can know; and adds: 'It is no explanation to say that the objective and subjective are two sides of one and the same phenomenon. Why should the phenomenon have two sides? This is the very core of the difficulty. There are plenty of molecular motions which do not exhibit this two-sidedness. Does water think or feel when it runs into frost ferns upon a window pane? If not, why should the molecular motion of the brain be yoked to this mysterious companion—consciousness?' [2]

Says Professor Tait, one of our most distinguished physicists: 'There are . . . things associated with living

[1] *Fragments of Science*, vol. ii. pp. 393, 394.
[2] *Ibid.* vol. ii. p. 410.

beings which, of course, no one in his senses can regard as physical. Even such things as consciousness and volition we have absolutely no reason, however vague, for classifying even in the smallest degree under the head of physics.'[1]

'I,' writes Professor Huxley, 'know nothing whatever, and never hope to know anything, of the steps by which the passage from molecular movement to states of consciousness is effected.'[2] And again, 'All our knowledge is a knowledge of states of consciousness. "Matter" and "force" are, so far as we can know, mere names for certain forms of consciousness.'[3]

Such disparity is there, then, between matter and mind, that it would be apparently as congruous to conceive of a thought as solidifying itself into a material object, as to conceive of any affection of material molecules as being the sole cause of thought. Hence, it follows that the Spencerian philosophy, which affirms the absolute distinctness of mind from matter, on the one hand; but, having no other structural elements *than* matter in motion, on the other hand, seeks to educe mind from these, is surely incongruous, and fails.

The demand is, that the primal atoms of the cosmic cloud, without a single logically added agent besides, have, by combining and recombining, by changing size and shape and intensifying the complexity of their motions, at last emerged into 'I am,' 'I can,' 'I ought;' that in effect they have written Faust and Hamlet, produced philosophies, discovered gravitation, calculated eclipses, realized the eternal

---

[1] *Recent Advances in Physical Science*, p. 70.
[2] *Contemporary Review*, Nov. 1871: 'Mr. Darwin and his Critics.'
[3] *Lay Sermons*, p. 373.

nobility of right and the eternal baseness of wrong: in brief, have brought about the moral and intellectual manhood that is ours. What we *know* by scientific evidence is this: that the persistence of force makes the relations of matter and force permanent. Says Faraday: 'A particle of oxygen is ever a particle of oxygen, nothing can in the least wear it. If it enters into combination and reappears as oxygen—if it pass through a thousand combinations, animal, vegetable, mineral — if it lie hid for a thousand years and then be evolved—it is oxygen with its first qualities, neither more nor less. It has all its original force, and only that.'[1]

Then, in all the area of the universe as we know it, that is, within the range of our experience and experiment, infinite vicissitude leaves what we know as an elementary body, with its first qualities intact, neither more nor less. But we must transcend experience, disregard the evidence before us, and *believe* that if we give the primal atoms with their inalienable motion *time enough*, they will emerge at last, not only as life, but as intellect!

Can it avail to repudiate materialism, and yet to philosophically conjure mind out of matter? We must indeed recast our definition of matter to do this; but how? Says Professor Max Müller: 'Mill declares in one place (*Logic* v. 3, 3) that it is a mere fallacy to say that matter cannot think. Here again he ought to define first of all what he means by matter, and according to his definition it may or may not be a fallacy to say that matter cannot think. If we say that matter cannot think, we do not say so because we cannot conceive thought to be annexed to any

[1] *Philosophical Mag.*, iv. 13, p. 235.

arrangement of material particles ... the reason why we are justified in saying "matter cannot think" is our having in our language and thought separated matter from thought, our having called and conceived what is without thought matter, and what is without matter thought. Having done this, we are as certain that our matter cannot think as that $A = A$ and not $= B$.'[1]

The verdict of consciousness is the immovable base of all mental action. Our consciousness affirms our personality and insists on our identity. The Ego is conscious of itself as the hidden thread of unity on which are strung all the past and present states of consciousness and thought. Separate 'states of consciousness' as affections of matter we have seen are impossible. But even if they could exist, *to whom* is their existence? A pang of unutterable remorse, a thrill of keenest pleasure, do not feel themselves. I feel them; what is that I, to whom the feeling is? It is always there, and in the language of Spencer already quoted 'is the unknown permanent *nexus* which is never itself a state of consciousness, but which holds all states of consciousness together.' Then it is as real and more absolute than the 'states of consciousness' themselves.

The personal pronouns are as plentiful in the language of modern materialists as in the language of sentiment or theology. What do they represent?

Looking back and looking forward, thinking of 'what might have been' and anticipating what will be; and being absolutely conscious that it is 'I' in unchanged and unchanging identity that am looking back upon myself, and looking forward to myself, is unthinkable, unless

[1] *The Science of Thought*, p. 616.

something to which all successive states of consciousness have been, are, and shall be, is admitted. If I deny the separate existence of the Ego, I to all intents and purposes deny that I am, and yet it is I that am there, perjuring myself by the denial.

Not only is there consciousness and thought, memory and prevision, power and volition; but the person, the identity that is conscious and thinks, that remembers and anticipates, that is able and that wills, is an inextinguishable factor of being. And for this there is no provision in the formula of the Spencerian Philosophy.

True, as we have seen, it is fain to admit, outside its formula, the existence of a permanent somewhat lying beneath and outlasting all the flow of mental states; that it has always existed, that it must exist for evermore; that it is a 'power' sometimes identified with 'force;' but it is contended that this is infinitely and for ever unknowable. With this we cannot be concerned; in practice it is an abstraction equal to nothing. But it is no element of our analysis; it is no factor of the formula which contained the only data required by this philosophy to construct the universe. We cannot assume that this power was the cause of matter, or the cause of motion; for we are shown that we can know nothing concerning it. But this also is of no moment; for matter, motion, and the combinations they bring about, over countless millenniums of time, clearly understood, and fully interpreted, are supposed to contain in themselves, the explanation of all that is. But surely the promise of this philosophy is unfulfilled, its pledge is broken; it left its formula at the very outset of its career, and has employed structural principles, which to *it*, are absolutely alien.

Then to affirm that mind does not exist is impossible; to affirm that matter gave origin to mind is a contradiction. There is but one alternative: it is, that in the beginning, mind, acting through and in matter, by immutable and perfect modes, through unmeasured time, caused matter to assume its forms and display its phenomena; and, being mind, imparted mind to the universe wherever it is found: crowning all, in the moral and intellectual nature of man.

Thus the ultimate demand of thought, of reason, and of consciousness, is that when we are unravelling the modes of phenomena, pushing our inquiries into the conditions of all existences, generalizing vast areas of knowledge, expressing in formula of geometry and numbers the splendid rhythm and order of all things in heaven and earth, we are simply finding, and expressing, the thoughts of an Infinite Intelligence; discovering the modes by which His immutable perfections were caused to take form in matter and mind.

It is science alone that can discover and express the *mode* of action; it is theology alone that must strive reverently to lead the mind up from the mode, not to the *conception*, but to the inevitable existence and thought of the Creator.

In doing this, to suppose that there are no intellectual difficulties is to manifest narrow mental grasp; but there are no absolute contradictions; no incongruities intolerable to the mind. True, as we have seen above, we encounter the inevitable fact of the uncreate existence of the Infinite. But we have seen that this, though infinitely impenetrable by us for ever, is still not repugnant to our reasoning and moral faculties. Indeed the eternal existence of *matter* as not requiring proof is one of the assumptions of some materialists. But surely the self and necessary existence of an intelligent omnipotence is without measure more congruous. It has been argued that the eternity of matter is thinkable, because matter is immutable — retains its properties through every vicissitude conceivable in time and space. But surely gravity is an indispensable quality of matter; yet take a bar of iron, weighing a thousand pounds at the sea level, four miles high, and it loses two pounds of its weight; carry it to the distance of the moon from the earth, and it weighs but five ounces; and at a distance which could be computed its gravity would be absolutely lost. It is conceivable that all the 'modes of motion' by which matter is known to us, might, if we knew enough concerning them, be found to have conditions in which they would cease to operate. We must know that matter *is* unchangeable before the argument is valid. But even then it is incompetent.

What the mind asks, is power and intelligence, to account for the majesty of the universe, and the existence of mind; and if their cause, to be such, must be admitted to be uncaused, the majority of reflective minds can accept this, and in doing so, can fairly rest, and fully hope.

But, this granted, the question shapes itself afresh, 'In the beginning what?' Had matter a coeval existence, an eternal being like God? or did He create it? bring, what to our senses is something, directly out of nothing? None dare answer. Both suggestions refuse to be dealt with by reason. But the incongruity of both might vanish like starlight in the dawn, if we knew *what* that is, which constitutes matter. It would, perhaps, make the Divine mind more immanent than we could dare to imagine. But it is easier without measure, judged of by our only source of knowledge, our own mental experience, to conceive of matter as a product of mind, than mind as a product of matter.

What, then, is it that the reverent mean by a 'creative act'? What is involved in the affirmation, 'In the beginning God created the heavens and the earth'? *Must* the answer be speculative? or does the evidence of Nature indicate a method? If the answer must be wholly speculative, it is without a shred of value. But if the *mode* of creation be a question of evidence, who are the witnesses? They are those who are students and masters of the *facts* of Nature. Willing or not willing, in the end, we *must* accept the facts of Science. What, from the very nature and constitution of our mind, we are bound to accept as truth, it would be a travesty of all morality to ignore, much more to reject.

What was gained to morals, or religion, by rejecting Galileo's demonstration of a revolving earth and a central sun? When Kepler demonstrated the laws of planetary motion, in the spirit of his age he was obliged to suppose that the direct motion of the planets was brought about by some spirit influence which he denominated 'immateriate species,' capable of overcoming the inertia of material bodies. But the splendid insight of Newton enabled him to perceive, that the laws of planetary motion, were a consequence of the cosmical law of gravitation. This took the moving planets out of spirit hands, and reduced the music of their motions to a method—a mechanical 'law.' To thousands that was deemed a truce to 'atheism;' but it is an unalterable truth; and men yet believe in God.

Within the range of living memory it has been held as

vital to the existence of theology that creation, from the stars that fringe the margin of the universe, to the earth, and the crown of manhood, arose in six literal days. But science, with no weapon but inexorable fact, has made this for ever untenable. But the foundations of religion are unshaken.

Science has removed whole regions and æons of phenomena, from what was considered the supernatural, to the natural; but to believe that this is so much lost to theology is a feeble and faithless fallacy.

That conception of the Great Creator which takes its rise in the majestic law of universal gravitation must be sublimer than that which thought of Him as telling off spirits to move, and bear up the planets, in their paths.

Can that be a higher view of an illimitable Creative Mind, which conceived of Him as a Power who caused the earth to be formed, and the heavens to be filled, in six literal days, rather than to think of Him to whom there can be no yesterday and no to-morrow, but an unchanging now, as determining laws and forces, which, in the slow progression of uncounted ages, should express His creative will and accomplish His Divine idea?

I have read in vain, I have thought in vain, to understand what to later theologians was the method and the meaning of a creative act. 'Order is heaven's first law;' and law—method—is the very pulse of order. Surely creative action in matter could only have proceeded by law? It could only have been the prevision and predetermination, by the inscrutable Creator, of definite affections of matter by force, issuing in rhythmic motions and cosmic harmonies, which, by their progress through immeasurable time, should accomplish the creative purpose. 'Let there be light;' that is the equivalent, in human thought, of an incomprehensible Divine volition. 'And there was light,' that is, in human phrase, the affirmation of its historic accomplishment. But to those who know, as we at present do, the science of light, what time, what power, what majesty of method, did its perfect accomplishment involve!

'And God said, Let there be lights in the firmament of heaven.' That, in human phrase, and according to human modes of thought, expresses the mysterious intent of Almighty Mind to fill space with the splendour we see; and to people it with intelligence of which we can form no faintest vision. 'And it was so,' that is the record of the realized intent. But how realized? Not by a material actor who

> 'Rounded in his palm those spacious orbs,
> And bowled them flaming through the dark profound.'

That is impossible to thought; a travesty of the sublimer conceptions possible, even to finite minds. Then do we conceive them as, in our human sense, leaping into existence, and place and relation and motion and order? All our knowledge repudiates this merely human conception.

The only conception we can justly form is, that in the awful mystery of creative action, Divine will determined law, modes of affection of matter by motion, through force: making the dome of heaven and the peopled earth the realized will of the Eternal.

'And God said, Let the earth bring forth the living creature after his kind.' That is the utterance of the human conception, which can alone represent to us the Divine resolve to fill the earth with life—and the joy of living things. 'And it was so.' But what epochs of countless ages filled the incalculable interval! What life on life, through age on age, moved in stately march from the lower to the higher, while the rocks kept imperishable record! The facts of geology, so far as they carry us, are more accurate and certain than any records of human history. And the irresistible lesson taught by the accurate study of the fossil flora and fauna, from the dawn of the Laurentian epoch, is a persistent and upward unfolding of life-forms by law; and the operation of the law is as manifest, as the operation of the law of increasing adaptation is visible, in a historical study of naval architecture, from the first rude plank, the dangerous raft, right up, through all increasing adjustments and improved design, to the latest ship with stately curves and splendid speed.

There is a sense indeed in which creation by evolution or development is taking place for ever around us. Development is evolution beginning at a fixed point; evolution is only development *ab initio*.

Every spore that unfolds itself into a fern, every seed that gives origin to another tenant of the forest, every egg that peoples earth or air or sea with another life, is an instance of development. It is only abbreviated evolution; evolution which gives a written record of its laws in every stage, down to the primitive ovum. There the record of the organism in itself ceases. The primitive ovum is a simple cell. The worm, the grayling, the eagle, the man, are evolved from such.

But can the egg unfold itself from this protoplasmic speck by any process save that of predetermined law and energy? Is not every law that shall act, and all the unchangeable power to enforce it, contained potentially in that globule of matter which we cannot see? Every change that is wrought, from the first that is discoverable, to the last that ensues, in the evolving egg, is one unbroken stream of method; force, with mandates, as it were, acting on matter, with special adaptations. Never did human mechanist strive more visibly to embody his prescribed purpose than do the progressive activities of the embryo lead straight to the final result. They did not, as movements, determine their own actions, or the actions of each other; they all lay together potentially from the first.

In this, if you will carry back the conception of Divine law and purpose to the beginning, and apply it to the incomprehensible majesty of the universe, I can see a miniature of suggestion as to the creative method.

Can it strip theology of one ray of the splendour of Deity, to find, from the evidence of nature, that He thought, and willed into action, the balanced forces and immutable laws, which were so related to each other, and to the foreseen requirements of onward and upward movement, that their progress is music, and their products are harmonies? —perfect adjustments—and, amidst ever-changing circumstances, ever-changing adaptations and self-adjusted design?

Can there be any splendour of the Infinite mind more ineffable and effulgent than the evidence, in His works, that in the beginning He determined the potency and prevision of all the life, and all the adaptations, that ever have emerged or can emerge?

Will it be urged that this one comprehensive law of creative action, with all its methods and potentialities complete in the beginning, must denude history of miracle?

must make all things inevitable sequences, and every outcome in nature through all time only what must be, when the moment for its emergence had come? And that therefore the unforeseen would be impossible. I submit that such an inference is not inevitable. The universe becomes one lasting act of the unsearchable but immanent Eternal. The power by which the self-adjusting mechanism of the universe acts, took its rise, and has its continuity, in Him.

A miracle, in its broadest aspect, is a wonderful event; something, which from the known course of phenomena, science could not previse. Science would stultify her past and make impossible her future, if she affirmed that the unprevised and marvellous could not happen. Says Professor Huxley: 'A miracle, in the sense of a sudden and complete change in the customary order of nature, is intelligible, can be distinctly conceived, implies no contradiction; and therefore, according to Hume's own showing, cannot be proved false by any demonstrative argument.'[1]

Our knowledge of the observed processes of nature erects no mental barrier to the occurrence of something never before observed. Miracles are not, it is now broadly admitted, dependent on science, but on *evidence* for their possibility and truth. Nay, more, it is conceivable that, what to us might be profoundly miraculous, might be the outcome of sheer and unmodified natural law.

If we could annul the interval of time between the great minds of the long past and bring them into direct and intelligent contact with the most marked victories of modern research and genius, what would be the effect? Let it be imagined that Aristotle or Plato could stand by while

[1] Huxley's *Hume*, p. 133.

Tyndall demonstrated to them in Athens, that they could hold direct and instant intercourse with a friend in India; or proved to them, that we can demonstrate the actual constituents of the sun and stars, and their physical conditions, with the same certainty as we can determine the analysis of an earthly compound; or bid the sunbeam paint the portrait of a bird or beast in rapid motion; or let them gaze upon the marvellous world of the minute unfolded by the modern microscope; and I do not hesitate to say that if he were the Aristotle or Plato of his own age, standing before these triumphs of this age, he would be standing in the presence of absolute miracles. Yet how have these, to Plato, unforeseen and wonderful events arisen? Only by discovery of, and absolute obedience to, the *laws of nature* as they are for ever and immutably acting. Man has created nothing, interrupted nothing, violated nothing: he has obeyed; and by obedience conquered.

Then grant that mind, by infinite wisdom and will, gave origin to this ever-unfolding universe, by methods that are all and for ever known to Him, as they can never be known to us, is it according to reason to contend that nothing shall ever happen *even according to the strict methods of natural phenomena* which past experience has never known?

That will happen, on the assumption of a Creative Mind as the origin of all, which is *needful*, to complete the universe; and what happens need be no interruption, no turning aside, of the course of nature, but only sublime compliance with it.

But more: one of the gravest conflicts of sheer material philosophy with Theism and Theology is, that by mechanical evolution design is swept clean from the universe; that teleology has received its death-blow.

Science finds that phenomena are self-acting, and self-adjusting. The energy is competent; the method is perfect for bringing about the result investigated. Science can find no more; it asks no more; and materialism says, there is no more. There is no design in it; it is, because to be at all, it must be that. There is no design in the form of the river-bed which the mighty waters have engraved for themselves in their irresistible movement down the mountain slope and along the windings of the valley to the sea. It is the result of the force of gravity. Such is the argument.

But while science as such, in strict obedience to its canons, must stop at the self-adjustment of immediate phenomena, and materialism will stop there, the reasoning faculties of the race, as we have seen, will not stop there. They must come at last, by the laws of reason, upon the power and the intelligence by which the methods of nature were made self-acting. Gravitation and the properties of water will account for the perfect adaptation of the river to its bed, and the bed to the purpose of a river. But how came gravity? How came the properties of water? There may be, there is, no direct design in the path of the Amazon or the Danube; but surely there is magnificence in the design that caused the great, the cosmic *methods* of nature so to co-operate as to cause those rivers inevitably to carve their perfect paths? The dynamics of nature are self-acting up to the very limit of our power of research; but after that, and beyond it, what? Why is the *direction* of nature's dynamical methods always and everywhere, through all time and space, beneficent and beautiful?

It is only the design, the teleology, of the old school, touched by the Ithuriel spear of modern knowledge, and changing into a conception of universal design, that can only have originated in an infinite mind.

The 'law of evolution' and that of 'variation and the survival of the fittest' may, if you will, be held to account for all that narrower knowledge had attributed to direct design. But evolution, like gravitation, is only a method; and the self-adjustments demonstrated in the 'origin of species' only make it, to reason, the clearer, that variation and survival is a method that took its origin in mind. It is true that the egg of a moth, and the eye of a dogfish, and the forearm of a tiger *must* be what they are to accomplish the end of their being. But that only shows, as we shade our mental eyes, and gaze back to the beginning, the magnificence of the design that was *in*volved in nature's beginning, so as to be *e*volved, by the designed rhythm of nature's methods.

Whatever matter may be; whatever force is; or whether or not both are the one inseverable product of omnipotent volition; the first affection of matter by force carried with it, potentially, the finished purpose of the All-wise, whatever that may be. Every instance of what such writers as Darwin are obliged to write of as 'contrivance' or 'adaptation' throughout this universe as it now is, or that shall yet arise in it through all duration, are, and will be, but factors of related harmony in a stupendously vast interlocked 'mosaic' of design, which in its entirety has a 'final purpose' too great for man to see.

It is admitted by the fullest and farthest thinkers, that the teleological, and the mechanical views, of phenomena and their origin, are not antagonistic. Instead of mutually excluding each other in thought, they are the complement of each other.

To argue, that because we can by analysis and research, discover and demonstrate the physical conditions or antecedents, that, apparently automatically, bring about a manifest contrivance, therefore, we have excluded the possibility of any universal primal design, is a mode of reasoning, the fallacy of which, surely, needs no great logical acumen to lay bare.

Because we discover the molecular shapes and movements that determine the structure of a beautiful crystal, it would be surely illogical and unwarranted to say that there was no design, no arrangement in the primary order of things, out of which these very conditions arose. It is conceivable that there may be infinitely more mind in the origination of that which automatically gives rise to a manifest 'contrivance,' than in directly originating it.

An ordinary watch, is, as a rule, a good timekeeper, under a fixed, say a temperate meridian; but take it to the arctic circle, and it goes too fast; or to the torrid zone, and it goes too slow. But in a chronometer, delicate compensations are made, of a beautiful kind, so contrived as to counteract the thermal changes. Would it be logical to think of the more complex contrivance as devoid of design because it is self-acting?

I grant that there may not be absolute parity of reasoning in the human as compared with the natural instance; but I only desire the reasoning to apply to one essential point. If primarily the methods of nature, which by their rhythmic action automatically produce contrivances, living

know of the Method of Creation. 63

or otherwise, took their origin in mind, the contrivances so produced were so designed to be produced; and this is contrivance of an infinitely higher order than the self-compensating balance of the chronometer. It is 'contrivances brought about by arrangements that are infinitely complex, transcending all thought; and which include in their vast sweep, all time, all space, all matter, all motion, and all their relations, from the most inconceivably minute phenomenon to the most stupendous that ever has happened, or can happen, as a product of nature.

We may easily reduce this to a practical form by illustration. The arm or fore-limb of all mammals is constructed essentially on the same type. The forearm of the horse is most highly specialized. In the forearm there is, as in the human skeleton, the *radius* and the *ulna*. But the ulna has lost its function, and is fused with the radius. What we call the knee in the horse's fore-limb is really the wrist. There are eight bones in the human wrist. The horse has only seven. Now, immediately succeeding the wrist bones in the human hand, are the five bones that form the palm; and these are followed by the five digits or fingers.

It appears, then, that, unlike the majority of mammal hands, the horse is peculiar. Instead of five bones corresponding to the palm bones, it has only one, which is called the 'cannon bone;' and this is followed by but one digit or finger with a huge nail. The horse then walks upon a single finger, viz. the third, on each fore foot and each hind foot. Why is this? and can we discover the history of this modification?

Examine the cannon bone of a horse with care; you will

find fixed on either side of it two delicate bones, called 'splints,' with actually no mission in the economy of the extant horse.

Now go steadily back in geological time. There are three great geological epochs, the primary, the secondary, and the tertiary. The recent period called the quaternary is a sub-section of the last. Now in the quaternary and upper tertiary, fossil horses are found. They correspond with the horses we see. But in the middle of the tertiary epoch we come upon the horse, not only in Europe, but in India, and above all in America, with the splint bones, that we find in extant horses fixed to the cannon bone, as long as that bone itself, and provided with small spurious or useless hoofs, while the ulna can be traced for its whole length.

In the earliest miocene deposits the horse is found with these spurious or partially aborted toes, no longer useless, but having the full length of the middle toe; making the horse of that epoch a distinctly three-toed creature, and each toe operative; while the forearm is in a condition normal to mammals.

Yet another form, found in America, shows, not only the three distinct and useful toes, but upon the third toe a splint, suggesting a rudiment of the little or fifth finger; while in the oldest of the tertiary rocks has again been found a horse with the fourth finger complete. While finally, in the very earliest tertiary deposits is found a horse with a foot of four perfect digits, consisting of the second, the third, the fourth, and fifth fingers, with a rudiment or splint of the first finger distinctly visible.

Similar facts reveal themselves in relation to the hind

feet and legs; and slow variations palpably affected the entire body of the successive types of horse; the teeth, for example, undergoing remarkable successive modifications: and whilst the *Eohippus* and the *Orohippus*, the last types of horse, discovered respectively in the oldest and later of the eocene beds, possess forty-four teeth, as in a large number of fossil and extant mammalian forms, the recent horse has the number reduced to forty, and their forms remarkably altered, as the final outcome of a succession of modifications.

We have here, then, a series of generic types; for the true relations of which to each other we are indebted to the insight of such workers as Huxley and Marsh and Lartet, and others. They do not afford us illustrations of the minute and scarcely observable modifications which the law of the origin of species involves; they present us rather with a series of family groups; but the relation between them is such as to leave the mind accustomed to biological investigations convinced, that, could we see all the forms that occurred between them, there could be no question as to the origin of these forms, from *eohippus* of the oldest eocene beds to *equus* of to-day. Unlike as in a general sense they are, they are progressive modifications, with higher and higher specializations, until, in the extant horse, the highest special modification is attained.

It will harmonize with no dogma of theology, and no doctrine of science, to assume that these equine forms, separated by such enormous epochs of time, were specially created: all accurate knowledge forbids the supposition; while varieties sufficiently marked, such as the race-horse, the giant and powerful dray-horse, the Shetland and the

Norman ponies, known to be derived from a common parentage, give the clearest sanction to the inference, that what we now know of the geological history of the horse proves it to be a product of the Darwinian law of evolution; that there has been no total destruction of equine (or any other) life in the great past; but that there has been a continuity of it, borne from region to region, and modified continuously by a thousand changing circumstances. Consequently we find, in the rocky records of the past, that organic types become simpler, and liker to each other, as we trace them through the incomplete geological record to a dim and far off age.

Here, then, we have a series of such generalized types, plainly related to each other in time, leading us down from the horse of historic times to less and less specialized forms of it, as the epoch grows more remote; until in the upper mesozoic or lower eocene beds, we find the progenitor of the line of the equine types we know, to be an animal with a splay foot of five toes, adapted to slow movement in a boggy soil. The slow specialization adapted it to increasing rapidity and ease of movement, and modified states of soil; acting, without doubt, as an increasing protection against its enemies, and providing it with an ever surer means of obtaining abundant and suitable food. And beneficial variation continued to act until the noble horse, beautiful in form, exquisitely graceful in action, and swift as the wind, had been thus created.

Now the most absolutely assured, the most universally accepted truth within the whole realm of human knowledge and experience is the immutability of nature's laws; and the certainty that their action has been 'established for ever' through all space and all time. Great as was the knowledge of ancient and classic peoples, that of which they knew relatively least, was nature. This arose from their inability to perceive the inexpressible vastness of nature, on the one hand, and the detailed constitution of the earth and its universal flora and fauna, on the other. The obvious inference as to the origin of the universe, as they knew it, was, that all that constituted the world and its occupants and inhabitants, mineral, vegetable, and animal, were individual direct creations. But, knowing as we now know, the immutability and universality of the laws of nature, in relation equally to the organic and living as to the inorganic and not-living, and knowing as we do the geological and palæontological history of the earth, and the nature and characteristics of its living inhabitants, it is as manifest as the axioms of geometry, that the direct and supra-natural creation of new species, or even new genera, is absolutely untenable.

Now modern biological science, guided by the splendid genius and ceaseless research of Darwin, and the whole field of biologists, for the past quarter of a century, has been able for all practical purposes to discover and demonstrate a great 'law' or method, according to which all the varieties of living 'species,' animal and vegetable, have arisen; connecting the remotest ages of the life of the globe with the present flora and fauna in one unbroken continuity, by one unchanging method. The organic history of any individual becomes an analogue of the organic history of the world. The individual begins existence as a minute ovum, and progresses to completeness. The vast series of organic forms, fossil and extant, began in one or more 'primordial germs.' The law of all living things, and especially the lowliest, is rapid and abundant reproduction. Variations in individuals so reproduced are as absolutely universal as reproduction itself. It does not require the accurate knowledge of the botanist or the zoologist to discover this. A careful study of any group of living forms, lowly or highly organized, will make this palpable to any observer. The septic organisms, for example, which arise from germs (not those which arise from self-division) constantly vary; and I have been able to make use of this tendency so as to enable three of these wonderful organic and vital specks to slowly change, so as to adapt themselves to changed environments, until, in the course of years, from normally living at a temperature of 60° Fahr. they lived at last, and multiplied enormously, at a temperature of 157° Fahr.; and in the slow process of adaptation, demonstrated fundamental changes were undergone by the organisms.[1]

A study of the Desmids, the Diatoms, the Radiolaria, or the Foraminifera amongst minute organisms will show that variations are so constant and so numerous, that the determination of what is called species, is difficult, and at times, impossible.

Who does not know of the varieties that are annually produced from seed-growths of favourite flowering plants? —the pelargonium, the primula, the viola, the rose, and hundreds of others.

That this is not confined to forms under cultivation is equally manifest. Common observation has not noted it perhaps, but there are no fewer than thirteen distinct forms

[1] *Journ. Roy. Micro. Soc.* 1887, President's Address.

of the common bramble or blackberry, with stem, flower, and fruit sufficiently varied to have induced some botanists to consider them species. Although each when seen is called by the majority of people 'the wild rose,' there are at the very least seventeen natural varieties. 'Artificial selection' has had no part in these variations and a thousand others that might be named.

Consider the variations constantly arising in fowls, canaries, dogs, and cattle. No litter of kittens is ever precisely alike, or precisely like either parent; and this is true even in human families.

Variation, then, is constant and universal; it acts in all directions and in every living thing. If, amidst the exigencies of the history of an organism, some variation in the progeny is beneficial in altered circumstances, it is by the very nature of things preserved. The offspring of all living organisms are greatly in excess of the number that can reach maturity; and with variations in every organism, and in every part of their organization, for ever occurring; and environments, during great cycles of time, undergoing constant and enormous changes; it is palpable that successive modifications must arise, and through all the countless ages of the past have arisen: resulting always in the 'survival of the fittest' or 'natural selection,' which 'signifies the preservation of favourable individual differences and variations, and the destruction of those which are injurious.'[1] This is palpable, for individuals possessed of advantage over others must have the best chance of surviving and multiplying their kind; hence arise 'varieties,' 'races,' and 'species;' and if the enormous age of the period of life upon the

[1] Darwin's *Origin of Species*, 6th ed. p. 63.

globe, and the vicissitudes through which it has passed, be taken into account, it is impossible for a biologist to withhold consent to the fact that a 'law,' a method, has been demonstrated, which has been a certain and powerful factor, in producing the variety of the flora and fauna that have filled the earth, from the dawn of life upon the globe, up to the extant animals and vegetables which are the latest outcome of this great law. This is the conviction of all the experts of the world.

That there are other factors of evolution not yet discovered is almost inevitable; they, however, will be but added 'laws;' supplementary and co-ordinated methods— giving greater completeness to our knowledge of the origin of species.

But having reached this conclusion, we are at once compelled to ask, What is the origin of this unceasing continuity of variation in all living things? this power to become constantly adapted to change of environment, and for ever, in the fittest form, to survive? Is not this palpably a creative method? Is it not the emergence in time and history of the thought and will of the Creative Power in the beginning?—one of the processes that lay enfolded in the very purpose of the production of heaven and earth, and which as a prevised method only awaited 'the fulness of time' to come inevitably into play?

The earth, as is well known, and we have already pointed out, is constantly subject to minute, as well as to smaller cyclic and great secular, changes. Nothing but an ability to become adapted through all duration to current and recurrent changes, could have made a continuity of the living population of the globe possible. We have found the principal 'law' of those adaptive changes. But because we have learned the nature of the law or method, by which throughout all time, these changes have been brought about; and because the method *appears* self-acting like the balance wheel of a chronometer, must we argue that there is no design either in the method or its results? That will not satisfy the constant demands of reason. Finding the law according to which a projectile moves, must not be confounded with the cause of its motion.

'Natural selection' cannot originate anything. Variation does not explain itself. Why is it a property of all living things to vary indefinitely and in all directions? The Darwinian law has no existence without it; but that 'law' no more accounts for this tendency, than the law of falling bodies explains gravitation, or shows why it acts as it does.

It is easy to explain the law of the compensations of a chronometer balance, or a compensating clock pendulum; but that does not account for their existence.

The law of 'inheritance,' the likeness of progeny to parents, is, like the law of variation, universal. But why is it so? If it were not so, there could be no survival of the fittest. Yet it is no more explained by the discovery of that law, than the nature of that which thinks, is explained by a discovery of the laws of thought.

Selection implies alternatives to select from. The splendid organic mechanism of all the animals of the earth, with their perfect relations to their sphere, could as a whole, only have been brought about by means that started for, and led to, that goal. 'The law by which structures originate is one thing; those by which they are restricted, directed, or destroyed is another.'[1]

Then, because the horse becomes specialized and adapted to its circumstances in a remarkable manner, leaving evidence in the rocks of long severed but successive epochs, of the very manner in which it was created as we know it; and because we have proof that this method is practically self-acting, shall we stultify reason by assuming that in its self-action there is no design? that as a great rhythmic law it had no origin? that, because to our powers of observation it is automatic, it explains its own existence? or that it strips the mind, by this very automatism, of any necessity for, or right of, having its origin explained? None of these assumptions are congruous; they surely violate the fundamental principles of thought.

We may be enabled no longer to say of any structure that it is a 'final cause;' our insight is not deep enough for that; but an equally powerful weapon in defence of theism takes its place: I designate it 'CONCURRENT ADAPTATION;' that is, *fitness*, for ever, throughout all time and all space; and fitness absolutely constant amidst all changes. Adaptation is universally concurrent with existence; and whether we have to account for it by sudden and unexplained action, or by the slow operation of laws, is a matter of no essential moment: *it is there.*

Nothing, for example, can be more certain, than the powerful influence exerted on the coloration and morphology of flowers, all over the earth, by the visits of insects. The insects assiduously visit flowers for food, or nectar; and by their visits the pollen of one flower is

[1] *Origin of the Fittest*, by E. D. Cope, p. 225.

carried to the stigmatic surface of another: so effecting cross fertilization. The contrivances for making insect agency efficient, are so numerous, so palpable, and so exquisitely perfect as to entrance the observer. One flower has its nectar in a tube, to reach which the proboscis of the visiting insect must touch and split a delicate tissue and expose the moist adhesive surfaces of a couple of pollen masses, which adhere to and are carried away by the insect, in such a position that, in visiting another flower of the same species, it must deposit the pollen where alone it can do its fertilizing work.

Another flower is so contrived, that to reach the nectar, the visiting insect must touch a sensitive surface causing the rupture of a tissue, which confines a pollen mass; but, on the rupture of the tissue, this flies out like an arrow at the unbidden guest; and an adhesive end sticks to the insect, which is startled away; but, visiting another flower of a like kind, deposits, in the right place, the fertilizing pollen it unconsciously carries.

Another flower has an ingenious arrangement by which it lures an insect into its corolla, and then imprisons it, provided with plenty of food, until its anthers are ripe, when it sheds their pollen over the insect; after which, by a special organic arrangement, it opens the prison door and lets its visitor emerge, charged with pollen, to visit another similar flower, which will inevitably be in a condition to receive fertilization from its pollen-covered body.

Thousands of other instances might be given.

Now we know perfectly the mutability of flowers. It is highly probable that the visiting insect and the visited flower were wholly unlike, in some instances, what they now are, twenty thousand years ago; and it is equally improbable that they will be what they now are, twenty thousand years hence. But that which this great biological law affirms, is, that whatever the changes, and however brought about, past or future, there never has been, there is not, and there never will be, an instant's cessation of concurrent adaptation :—the operation of the 'law' that secures to all that lives adjustment to its environments. That surely must be a method that took its origin in mind; and it must have had its prevised and pre-ordered place potentially assigned, from the earliest creative movement; as it must continue to have unceasing action to the very terminus of all organic existence.

Design, purpose, intention, appear, then, when all the facts of the universe are studied in the light of all our reasoning faculties, to be ineradicable from our view of the creation. Teleology does not now depend for its existence on Paleyean 'instances;' but all the universe, its whole progress in time and space, is one majestic evidence of teleology. The will and purpose running through it are as incapable of being shut out of our consciousness and reasoning faculties, as its phenomena and their modes are of being rendered wholly imperceptible by our senses.

A 'mind' that is not a mind, in any sense as we know it, is, to us, nothing. Will, to be will, to us, must be such as we know of; though it be infinite. Intelligence that is infinite cannot cease to be intelligence. To an infinite intelligence, as to us, in the same conditions, the properties of conic sections must be what we know them to be. But an Infinite Mind would differ absolutely from ours in that there could be nothing tentative, nothing experimental in its methods, through all time and space. Only the right means would ever be employed, or the right ends ever be brought about. But, surely, even an Infinite will, in the realm of matter, must *use* means. When human power takes a pebble from a great height and places it at the sea-level it has only done what gravity could have done. But when human will by continuity of purpose combines materials to form a calculating machine, we have an evidence of the action of mind; something, which, while it is made and exists by the very laws of nature, yet the laws of nature could not, by themselves, have made.

Similar results must be due, then, to similar conditions. The teleology, that is the inseverable motive, as it were, of all the activities and interactions of nature, must be the product of mind.

Then was *man*, as a physical being, the terminal link in the great progressive chain of living forms that had peopled the earth through countless ages? Or does he, in physical origin, stand apart? Is he a being from whose existence a new creative epoch dates? Or is he the final product of the vast ancestral line of life that ran through all the ages? Did God make man 'of the dust of the ground' by some process of which we can form no conception, and can discover no trace? Or is there evidence that the Creator made man of the dust of the ground by majestic laws, acting over vast epochs, until he had become meet for the inbreathing of a higher nature?

That is a question of profoundest interest. But if the authoritative and final demonstration were given either way to-morrow, we, in ourselves, should remain unaltered. We should be conscious of no uplifting and of no fall.

Immediate or mediate creation, if God be the author, must be alike Divine. To fear the consequences of honest truth seeking research on this momentous question, is to manifest little love of truth for its own sake, on the one hand; and little stalwartness of personal conviction, as to the security of the foundation of professed beliefs, on the other. Whether we will or not, the whole matter will be searched to its deepest depths. But amidst all the conflict of opinion as to details, in one thing all are agreed, and that is, that the gulf between man and the noblest apes is such as to be practically without comparison. Whatever science may be able to show ultimately as to the relation of man to the anthropoid apes, there is to-day no biologically demonstrated and direct kinship. That the anthropoid apes, as we know them, were in any proper sense the *direct* ancestors of man, is not a serious contention of even extreme evolutionists. The facts before us do not justify it. The highest ape is still an ape; and whilst the oldest human remains, such as the Engis and Neanderthal skulls, discovered in association with evidences of immense antiquity, have remarkable characteristics, pointing in some respects in the direction of the great apes, they are still the crania of men. After a critical and exhaustive examination of the two skulls above referred to, Professor Huxley says concerning the Eugis skull: 'Its measurements agree equally well with those of some European skulls. And assuredly there is no mark of degradation about any part of its structure. It is, in fact, a fair average human skull, which might have belonged to a philosopher, or might have contained the thoughtless brains of a savage.'[1] And in

[1] *Man's Place in Nature*, Huxley, p. 157.

summing up the results of an equally critical examination of the far more remarkable Neanderthal skull, the same unquestionable authority says: 'In no sense, then, can the Neanderthal bones be regarded as the remains of a human being intermediate between men and apes. At most they demonstrate the existence of a *man* whose skull may be said to revert somewhat towards the pithecoid type. . . . And indeed, though truly the most pithecoid of known human skulls, the Neanderthal cranium is by no means so isolated as it appears to be at first, but forms in reality the extreme term of a series leading gradually from it to the highest and best developed of human crania.'[1] Nothing has arisen to seriously modify these authoritative statements. No thorough anatomist practically familiar with the structure of the anthropoids on the one side, and man on the other, could attempt to argue that man can be directly a descendant of chimpanzee, gorilla, or orang. 'I may say,' says Huxley, 'that the fossil remains of man hitherto discovered do not seem to me to take us appreciably nearer to that lower pithecoid form, by the modification of which he has probably become what he is.'[2]

But let us beware of mistaking, or even distorting, the true meaning of this, as understood by the philosophical evolutionist. It does not for a moment place the physical nature of man outside the range of the great creative law of natural selection. No arrangement of the monkeys can present us with a rational order of development, of which man is physically the latest and highest outcome. But the precursor of man, of whose actual existence no direct proof has yet arisen, is assumed, on the evidence of absolutely

[1] *Man's Place in Nature*, Huxley, p. 157.   [2] *Ibid.* p. 159.

innumerable details, the full value of which is only to be clearly seen by experts, to have ascended, not from any anthropoid,—chimpanzee, gorilla, nor orang,—but these apes are found to form the nearest branch existing, produced by the same trunk, out of which, physically, man's nature was, by the law of descent, evolved.

That the embryological and anatomical resemblances between man and the highest apes are of a profound and striking character, no sane educated man would attempt to traverse; and that this involves close biological relationship, and proves the operation on each, of the same organic laws of development, so far as physical origin is concerned, is also certain.

That there are evidences of an antiquity of the human race, as such, immensely disproportionate to that indicated in the absolutely unreliable and useless 'received' chronologies, it would be folly to doubt and immorality to neglect. It is evidenced by man's works, which are shown, without question, to be of indefinitely vast antiquity; and correspond, in the main, with the works of races of men still living. It is shown by the enormous antiquity of races of men as we know them; by the vast age of languages, made evident, by a deep analysis of their structure, as sister and parent languages; as well as by the great age of even human remains.

Now all this, taken in connection with the anatomical structure and embryological development of man, makes it impossible to suppose that man's physical nature was not a product of the same great creative laws, the same vital processes, as those that gave origin to the chimpanzee or the gorilla; a slow creation, through a long line of varied life, from 'the dust of the ground,' the elements of the earth. There is in this relation an almost marvellous insight in David's song:—

> 'I will give thanks unto Thee; for I am fearfully and wonderfully made:
> Wonderful are Thy works;
> And that my soul knoweth right well.
> My frame was not hidden from Thee,
> When I was made in secret,
> And curiously wrought in the lowest parts of the earth.
> Thine eyes did see mine unperfect substance;
> And in Thy book were all my members written,
> Which day by day were fashioned,
> When as yet there was none of them.'[1]

By what link man is united physically to the great series below him, by what line and in what specific manner he arose, it has not yet been given to science to determine. Biological science sees, with inevitable certainty, that he must have been in vital union with that series; that physically he is a part of the majestic organic whole, from the first dawn of life upon the globe until now.

At the same time it is equally certain that other agencies which could not have acted on ape or other mammal, nor indeed on any other living form besides, came into operation, when man, as such, became an inhabitant of this earth.

Nor is it by any means other than conceivable that science, which has transformed the face of the world in fifty years, may be able to demonstrate the actual physical line of man's origin. But if that be so, if the line along which man's physical nature was moulded of the dust of the ground, by the Creative Mind and will, were made so plain that none could refuse the evidence, it may leave undisturbed our mental peace, and unaltered our conviction of the dignity

[1] Ps. cxxxix. vers. 14-16.

and majesty of man. It would leave our responsibilities undiminished, our rights uninfringed, and our hopes unclouded.

The saint is none the less saintly, because he is ancestrally the last, and prevised outcome, of an inconceivably grand progression of creative laws, operating through countless cycles, than he would have been, as the descendant of a man produced by an isolated act of creation. The song of the nightingale is no iota less rich in fluent melody because its larynx was modified from less melodious forms; and the martyrdom of Paul, or the noble sacrifices of heroes and reformers to secure the sacred rights of liberty and truth for their fellow-men, are none the less exalted because we must trace their ancestry to the slow operation of creative laws, which in the great unbroken stream of life upon the earth gave origin to the monod, the coral-polyp, the mollusc, the lizard, the aye-aye, and the chimpanzee. Verily, if the researches of science demonstrate that this was the method of creative action, we may not murmur.

The sovereignty of man does not depend on a particular view of the exact manner in which the Creator caused the elements of the earth to produce his frame. 'And the Lord God formed man of the dust of the ground;' it is not *how* He so formed him. None has power to affirm or to deny how, unless with reverent hands he find it written in the rocks, or woven indelibly with the very structure of man himself. It is because men have interpreted, without evidence, the stages of creative action, and welded these non-essentials with iron girdles of dogma, that faith has again and again been imperilled.

The true crown of manhood, the final majesty and exalted mystery of creative power, was not man's *body*, but his soul. 'And breathed into his nostrils the breath of life, and he became a living soul,' is the expression of that which gives his unshared dignity to man.

What is meant by this, who shall explain? Who can peer into the depths of a mystery so profound? It defies all our powers of search; dare we make a special interpretation or understanding of how this was brought about, an essential of belief? Is it not enough that it was the supreme, as it was, so far as our present knowledge will carry us, the final outcome of creation?

When the Creative Power and wisdom had built man's physical nature of the dust of the ground, whether suddenly or slowly, by this method or by that, He breathed into his nostrils the breath of life, and he became a living soul. It was the possession of what we call the soul that gave to the manhood its being. How this was imparted, who can know? who shall explain? Even if the very *method* be at last discovered, or approximated, the unalterable question must remain, *why* the method, the law, brought about so sublime a result, and from whence came the conditions that made the laws direct themselves to such an exalted end. In fine, how physical laws could so be caused to act as to give origin to consciousness, thought, and moral faculties. Plainly, this 'end' must have lain in the Divine 'beginning;' and we must go behind and below the mechanics of phenomena and explain their *vera causa*; we must find our way above matter not-living in the great past, and fathom the very essence of the cause that made it live, before we can attempt to explain the origin of that self in man which looks upon and *knows itself*. We have seen that matter and force will not, as sole factors, lend themselves to a philosophy of the origin and explanation of this. A linear arrangement of the ascending mentality of brutes does not really explain, or even minimize, the difficulties of the problem. It simply makes the area of the problem the wider.

'I am,' 'I can,' 'I ought,' 'I think,' with equal freedom—of an atom or a universe, of a rosebud or a Deity, of myself or of my race, of the grandeur of right and the baseness of wrong—these are the impenetrable mysteries which no property known to us in matter, and no process ever seen by us in matter and force, can ever *explain*.

No doubt the most profound and active minds amongst men will always endeavour to correlate the access even of mind, with modifications of cerebral and neural matter. But if that be approximately done, the real problem will remain simply untouched. True, we can afford no better explanations than those which philosophy offers; but we may not blind ourselves to the true value of these. Mind is inseverably associated with neural matter; we do not know, and cannot even think of it, as emerging as a product of neural matter. We must distinguish clearly between scientific evidence and plausibilities of a philosophical kind expressed in scientific language. We shall be fascinated again and again with a brilliant intellectual arrangement of things known, with things guessed, leading to hypothetical 'interpretations' of the most impenetrable mysteries. But the fact remains, that the activities of intellect are inexpressible in terms of matter and motion. Mind only can give origin to mind. Until it is congruous to think that parallel lines can enclose a space, that $2 + 2 = 7$, that out of nothing something can come, it will be incongruous, in spite of subtle and ceaseless effort, to construct hypotheses by which y shall by its own act change into x, or, in other words, by which mind, with its absolute disparity to matter, shall come forth as an unaided and necessary product of matter as affected by motion.

www.ingramcontent.com/pod-product-compliance
Lightning Source LLC
Chambersburg PA
CBHW020301090426
42735CB00009B/1177